T0278328

*The 500 Hidden Secrets of*

# SEATTLE

# INTRODUCTION

This book encourages you to explore Seattle from end-to-end, especially inviting you to venture out of the downtown tourist corridor. That's not to say that there's nothing special to be found downtown, as there are plenty of great restaurants, experiences and tucked away gems for the thoughtful visitor to enjoy. But to experience the best of this city, you need to spend time in the places where locals live and enjoy themselves, especially outside, rain or shine.

This edition of *The 500 Hidden Secrets* includes a new chapter on outdoor adventure. Even the most dedicated city folks will find themselves admiring nature while visiting Seattle and the Pacific Northwest. It's hard not to, when evergreen trees, snow-capped mountains, the Pacific Ocean and plenty of freshwater lakes beckon around every corner. Take at least one stroll along the water or in a city park while you are here to understand why so many people, including this author, can't possibly imagine living anywhere else.

This guide does not cover everything there is to do or enjoy in Seattle. It is designed as a source of inspiration with categories tailored to help you find a great experience suited to your interests while you are visiting. The author has long shared many of these favorite places with visiting friends and family and is happy to share them with you now, too.

# HOW TO
# USE THIS BOOK

———

This guide lists 500 things you need to know about Seattle in 100 different categories. Most of these are places to visit, with practical information to help you find your way. Others are bits of information that help you get to know the city and its habitants. The aim of this guide is to inspire, not to cover the city from A to Z.

The places listed in the guide are given an address, including the neighborhood (for example Capitol Hill or Ballard), and a number. The neighborhood and number allow you to find the locations on the maps at the beginning of the book: first look for the map of the corresponding neighborhood, then look for the right number. A word of caution however: these maps are not detailed enough to allow you to find specific locations in the city. You can obtain an excellent map from any tourist office or in most hotels. Or the addresses can be located on a smartphone.

Please also bear in mind that cities change all the time. The chef who hits a high note one day may be uninspiring on the day you happen to visit. The hotel ecstatically reviewed in this book might suddenly go downhill under a new manager. The bar considered one of the best cocktail bars might be empty on the night you visit. This is obviously a highly personal selection. You might not always agree with it. If you want to leave a comment, recommend a bar or reveal your favorite secret place, please visit the website *the500hiddensecrets.com* – you'll also find free tips and the latest news about the series there – or follow *@500hiddensecrets* on Instagram or Facebook and leave a comment.

# THE AUTHOR

Allie Tripp has lived in Seattle for just over a decade. What was supposed to be a short residency for graduate school turned into a love affair that is on track to continue for a lifetime. Being a 'transplant' has given her a tourist's eye for the city while her own travels around the world remind her what an important role a good recommendation can play when in a new place.

Her advice for enjoying your time as much as possible? Plan a day where you do one thing you know you'll love, try one thing that's new to you, and seek out at least one scenic vista. Watching the sun set over the Olympic Mountains is a particularly fond pastime of hers.

The author is immensely grateful for the many friends and colleagues who have helped inspire this list of 500 wonderful places in and around Seattle. Thanks especially to her husband, there's no one else she'd like to explore Seattle (or the world) with more. Thanks to her mother, father, sister, cousin and extended family and friends, whose many visits over the years built the foundation of this book. Many thanks are also due to her dear friend Millie, who introduced her to the *Hidden Secrets* series in Munich and was the cheerleader for this project from the very start!

She also wants to thank the team at Luster, especially Dettie Luyten for her support and dedication to this book. Extra gratitude is also due to her friend Alena Sullivan, whose beautiful photography graces many pages of this book. See more of her work at *burnashburn.com*.

# SEATTLE

*overview*

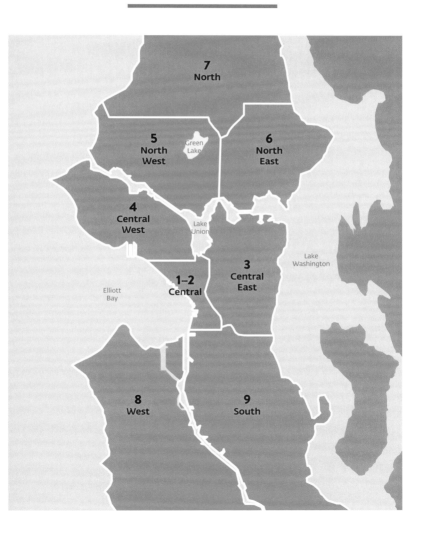

# Map 1
# CENTRAL (NORTH)

*Lower Queen Anne, Seattle Center, South Lake Union, Belltown, Downtown*

Lake Union

305

299

Lake Union
Park

255

398

256

Mercer St

**South Lake
Union**

51

139

Westlake Ave N

14

Fairview Ave N

175

172

I-5 Express

451

Denny Park

94

Denny Wy

158

152

6th Ave

4th Ave

5th Ave

268

**Belltown**

61

Stewart St

**Downtown**

58

429

313

455

8

440

452

88

150

Olive Wy

21

Pine St

1st Ave

Pike St

# Map 2
# CENTRAL (SOUTH)
## Pike Place Market, Downtown, Pioneer Square

# Map 3

## CENTRAL EAST

*Montlake, Arboretum, Madison Park, Capitol Hill, First Hill, Madison Valley, Madrona, Central District, International District*

EAT — **DRINK** — SHOP — BUILDINGS — DISCOVER — **CULTURE** — OUTDOOR — CHILDREN — SLEEP — WEEKEND — RANDOM

# Map 4
# CENTRAL WEST
*Magnolia, Interbay, Queen Anne, Westlake*

# *Map 5*
# NORTH WEST

### *Sunset Hill, Ballard, Greenwood, Phinney Ridge, Green Lake, Fremont, Wallingford, Northlake*

# Map 6
# NORTH EAST

*Wedgwood, Sand Point, Roosevelt, Ravenna,*
*University District (UDistrict)*

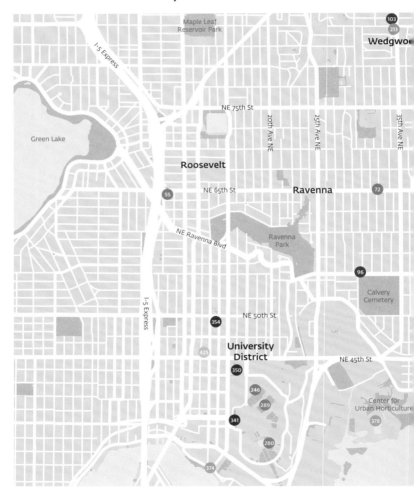

# Map 7
# NORTH

*Broadview, Bitter Lake, Crown Hill, Greenwood, Northgate*

# Map 8
# WEST

## Alki, North Admiral, The Junction, West Seattle, Highland Park, White Center

# *Map 9*
# SOUTH

*SoDo, North Beacon Hill, Mt. Baker, Columbia City, Georgetown,
Hillman City, Seward Park, South Park, Dunlap, Rainier Beach*

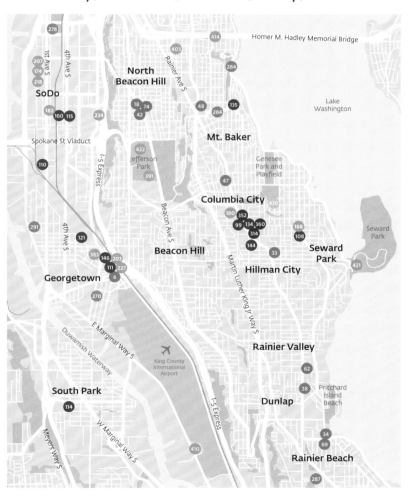

SALTY'S ON ALKI

# 85 PLACES TO EAT OR BUY GOOD FOOD

5 classic **SEATTLE BITES** —————— 24

5 hip restaurants **FOR A DATE** —————— 26

5 **FAMILY-FRIENDLY** restaurants —————— 29

The 5 best **BREWPUBS** —————— 31

5 spots from **FAMOUS SEATTLE CHEFS** —— 34

5 great places for **SEAFOOD** —————— 36

5 delicious **BAKERIES** —————— 38

5 **IMMIGRANT-RUN** restaurants —————— 40

5 spots **FIT-FOR-FOODIES** —————— 43

5 **WARM MEALS** for a cold night —————— 45

5 great **VEGETARIAN & VEGAN** eats —————— 47

5 locally loved **QUICK EATS** —————— 49

5 spots for Seattle **DONUTS** —————————— 51

5 places to satisfy your **SWEET TOOTH** —————— 53

5 meals to **START YOUR DAY** —————————— 56

5 **FOOD TRUCKS** worth finding————————— 58

5 Seattle **RESTAURANT INSTITUTIONS** ——— 60

# *5 classic*
# SEATTLE BITES

---

1 **SUSHI:**
**SUSHI KASHIBA**

86 Pine St, Suite 1
Downtown ②
+1 206 441 8844
*sushikashiba.com*

Chef Shiro Kashiba opened Seattle's first sushi bar in 1970 in the International District (inside Maneki, which still operates today). Sushi Kashiba is his third restaurant in the city and absolutely a must-visit for sushi lovers. The set dinners will allow you to enjoy the freshest, chef-selected options, though they will come at a price. Reservations are a must for this Pike Place hot spot.

2 **FUSION FOOD:**
**REVEL**

401 N 36th St
Fremont ⑤
+1 206 547 2040
*revelseattle.com*

There are quite a few candidates for 'classic bites' at Revel, but the Dungeness crab noodles with seaweed, red curry and *crème fraîche* just cannot be passed up. This Korean-influenced restaurant moved into new, larger digs in Fremont a few years ago and still manages to be full most of their open hours. Make a reservation and don't skip the cocktails or the kimchi.

## 3 CHEESE: BEECHER'S CHEESE

1600 Pike Place
Downtown ②
+1 206 956 1964
*beechershandmade
cheese.com*

Beecher's Handmade Cheese first opened in Pike Place Market in 2003 and has been delighting dairy fans ever since. You can view the cheesemaking kitchen through enormous windows on Pine Street. If you miss your chance to try some while you're at Pike Place, there's now an outpost at SeaTac airport and the cheese curds travel particularly well.

## 4 SEATTLE DOGS

Various locations

A Seattle dog is a hot dog topped with cream cheese and sautéed onions, often served in a pretzel bun. Yes, it sounds a little weird, and yes, it is very good. The first ever Seattle dog was created by Hadley Long at his bagel dog cart in Pioneer Square in 1989. We recommend trying one near Lumen Field or T-Mobile Park on a game day.

## 5 RAMEN: RAMEN DANBO

1222 E Pine St,
Suite 1
Capitol Hill ③
+1 206 566 5479
*ramendanbo.com*

Ramen is a popular Japanese noodle soup dish that is exactly what most Seattleites want on a cold, rainy winter evening. Ramen Danbo is a chain from Japan that first exported its excellent ramen to Vancouver, BC, and now Seattle. They offer traditional Tonkotsu ramen crafted in the Kyushu Hakata style, one of the most popular types in Japan.

# 5 hip restaurants
# FOR A DATE

6  **CIUDAD**
   6118 12th Avenue S
   Georgetown ⑨
   +1 206 7172 984
   *ciudadseattle.com*

Go here with foodie friends or dates who like to share and eat meat. The small plate menu is Mediterranean-influenced and allows for plenty of variety. All their meats are grilled to perfection over a charcoal grill you pass by as you enter the restaurant. Their industrial dining room is brightened up with colorful seating and an intriguing mural.

7  **COMMUNION**
   2350 E Union St
   Central District ③
   +1 206 391 8140
   *communionseattle.com*

Chef Kristi Brown's Communion took the Seattle food scene by storm when it opened in 2020, offering American soul food with PNW influences. The stylish interior matches their request that guests pop on their 'fancy threads' to visit. Enjoy the chicken special that changes daily, the BBQ shrimp and don't miss the mac and cheese.

6 CIUDAD

## 8   LIST RESTAURANT

2226 1st Avenue
Belltown ①
+1 206 441 1000
listbelltown.com

If you want to encourage a date to order everything (and anything) they want, take them to List for happy hour. The limited menu and stylish interior are perfect for a second or third date, and surrounding Belltown provides plenty of people watching if you sit on the balcony in nice weather. All bar food is 50% off at happy hour and bottles of wine are only 22 dollars.

## 9   BLACK BOTTLE

2600 1st Avenue
Belltown ①
+1 206 441 1500
blackbottleseattle.com

This minimalist, stylish gastrotavern focuses on shared plates that come out as soon as they are ready and a well-curated bar list. The menu has plenty to offer palates of all kinds, including those with varying dietary restrictions, though the squeaky halloumi cheese hasn't left the menu in a decade for a reason.

## 10   KEDAI MAKAN

1449 E Pine St
Capitol Hill ③
+1 206 535 3562
kedaimakansea.com

This Capitol Hill favorite recently came under new management that promises to honor the reputation this restaurant has built around serving Malaysian-inspired street food. The Malay peanuts are the perfect accompaniment to your beverage of choice. Their new reservation policy makes it easier to get a table exactly when you want one.

# 5 **FAMILY-FRIENDLY**

## *restaurants*

---

11 **FRĒLARD PIZZA COMPANY**
4010 Leary Way NW
Fremont ⑤
+1 206 946 9966
*ethanstowell
restaurants.com/
locations/frelard-
pizza-company*

This Ethan Stowell pizza joint has ample indoor and outdoor seating, great for families who don't want to feel cramped in close quarters. Their New York-style pizza has some inventive combinations (carbonara pizza!) and seasonal offerings. They host a good sampling of local breweries on their tap list for adults.

11 FRĒLARD PIZZA COMPANY

## 12 SERENDIPITY CAFE

3222 W McGraw St
Magnolia ④
+1 206 282 9866
*serendipitycafe
andlounge.com*

This homey, neighborhood spot in Magnolia has ample options for everyone in your party no matter the time of day. They serve a great breakfast here, but the lunch and dinner options also abound. There's a larger-than-normal kids' menu and a play area for youngsters with books and games.

## 13 THE EGG & US

4609 14th Avenue NW,
#108
Ballard ⑤
+1 206 402 3080
*theeggandus.com*

Sometimes you just need a classic diner breakfast. The Egg & Us is the perfect balance of homey atmosphere (the decor showcases the coloring activities available for kids of all ages) and classic, well-executed breakfast fare. Don't overlook the Mexican-influenced menu options.

## 14 PORTAGE BAY

391 Terry Avenue N
South Lake Union ①
+1 206 462 6400
*portagebaycafe.com*

With five locations, this local standout isn't *quite* a secret anymore, but it is worth visiting because the quality is consistently excellent and the menu is expansive enough to suit any picky eater's palate. The breakfast part is particularly fun for kids who can handle the responsibility of serving themselves.

## 15 WING DOME

7818 Greenwood
Avenue N
Greenwood ⑤
+1 206 706 4036
*thewingdome.com*

Looking for a place to bring the kids and also catch a few game highlights? Wing Dome in Greenwood feels like a sports bar for families, with plenty of TVs, excellent wings, and friendly service. The kids' menu is reasonably priced, but depending on the young person's palate, they might want to sample all the great wing sauces like a grown-up, too.

# *The 5 best* **BREWPUBS**

## 16 ELLIOTT BAY BREWPUB

4720 California
Avenue SW
The Junction ⑧
+1 206 932 8695
*elliottbaybrewing.com*

Elliott Bay Brewing Company has three locations, but we're here to recommend their original location in West Seattle. The wood-paneled pub is right on the main drag in Alaska Junction and is a great place to stop for a pint while you're exploring, or tuck in for a hearty meal. The steak and cheese sandwich is particularly good, especially paired with their Alembic Pale Ale.

## 17 BROUWER'S CAFE

400 N 35th St
Fremont ⑤
+1 206 267 2437
*brouwerscafe.com*

Modeled after the large-scale brew houses of Europe, you can't quite believe the size of Brouwer's when you first walk in. They host 60+ beers on tap and whiskeys from the Single Malt Scotch Society. Pair your beverage with *pommes frites* and ample dipping sauces or one of the other Belgian-inspired entrees.

18 PERIHELION BREWERY

18 **PERIHELION BREWERY**

2800 16th Avenue S
North Beacon Hill ⑨
+1 206 200 3935
*perihelion.beer*

Just a block from the Beacon Hill light rail station, this brew pub makes up for its limited indoor seating with some great patio setups, including fire tables and cheerful service. The food offerings are primarily great sandwiches (try the blackened salmon) and lots of sides and shareables. Perihelion's beers are on the funkier end; saison fans will enjoy themselves.

19 **MCMENAMINS SIX ARMS**

300 E Pike St
Capitol Hill ③
+1 206 223 1698
*mcmenamins.com/
six-arms*

McMenamins is a name you'll hear in the Pacific Northwest if you explore enough. Each of the family-owned pubs, hotels and music venues has its own distinct history, and several of the locations are in rehabilitated historic properties, including this one. You can read all about the building's history while sipping a beverage and people watching out the large windows.

20 **THE PIKE BREWING COMPANY**

1415 1st Avenue
Downtown ②
+1 206 622 6044
*pikebrewing.com*

After you've spent the morning exploring downtown Seattle, pop into Pike Brewing Company for a classic pub fare lunch and a pint. The pub is adorned with plenty of Seattle and beer industry paraphernalia, keep an eye out for many neon signs. We recommend the Kilt Lifter, a quality Scotch ale, though the Mountain's Out IPA is worth buying in a can for the great design alone.

# 5 *spots from* FAMOUS SEATTLE CHEFS

21 **SERIOUS PIE**

**2001 4th Avenue**
**Belltown** ①
**+1 206 838 7388**
*seriouspieseattle.com*

With plenty of Tom Douglas restaurants to choose from, Serious Pie is our pick for its delicious pizza that showcases local ingredients (especially Penn Cove clams). Don't miss out on the kale salad or the happy hour at the downtown location. Two additional locations are in Ballard and Totem Lake.

22 **TAKU**

**706 E Pike St**
**Capitol Hill** ③
**+1 206 829 9418**
*takuseattle.com*

Famous for his stint on *Top Chef*, Shota Nakajima brings Osaka to Capitol Hill at Taku. The late-night menu is especially tantalizing after you've spent the evening bar hopping in Seattle's best nighttime neighborhood. You really can't go wrong with your order here, be sure to try as many sauces as you can.

## 23 HOW TO COOK A WOLF

2208 Queen Anne
Avenue N
Queen Anne ④
+1 206 838 8090
*ethanstowel
lrestaurants.com/
locations/how-to-cook-
a-wolf*

Ethan Stowell's How to Cook a Wolf is a stylish Seattle institution serving upscale Italian food. It's a spot to bring a date you want to impress. With two locations to choose from, we prefer this one as an excuse to explore the top of Queen Anne, which is especially charming around the winter holidays.

## 24 THE WALRUS & THE CARPENTER

4743 Ballard
Avenue NW
Ballard ⑤
+1 206 395 9227
*thewalrusbar.com*

Renee Erickson, a locally raised James Beard award-winning restaurateur and chef, owns a number of Seattle institutions that are all worth checking out. The Walrus & the Carpenter, which she started with two friends, stands out for its excellent local oyster selection, stylish interior and can't-go-wrong menu that changes daily. Build a stop in here for happy hour after an afternoon of exploring Ballard Avenue.

## 25 JOULE

3506 Stone Way N
Fremont ⑤
+1 206 632 5685
*joulerestaurant.com*

Rachel Yang & Seif Chirchi are a wife and husband duo that helm Relay Restaurant Group. Yang's Korean upbringing is the backbone of their cuisine with worldwide fusion influences. Joule is the more meat-focused of their two restaurants while sister restaurant, Revel, is better suited for seafoodies. Both dining options have innumerable mouthwatering bites (and cocktails).

# 5 great places for **SEAFOOD**

**26 MASHIKO**

4725 California
Avenue SW
The Junction ⑧
+1 206 935 4339
*mashikorestaurant.com*

This small but meticulously managed sushi restaurant in West Seattle has a sign on the front door noting that they open at 5:03 pm each day (except Tuesdays). Their focus on sustainability is tireless. We recommend splurging on the Omakase – you won't regret it.

**27 TAYLOR SHELLFISH OYSTER BAR**

1521 Melrose Avenue
Capitol Hill ③
+1 206 501 4321
*taylorshellfishfarms.com*

Taylor Shellfish has been farming oysters in the PNW since 1890, and their expertise shows. All of their three Oyster Bars are stylish, but the Capitol Hill location adjacent to Melrose Market is their original location and feels particularly hip. Order the Shucker's Dozen and a glass of bubbly or lemonade and savor one of the best bites the PNW has to offer.

**28 PACIFIC INN PUB**

3501 Stone Way N
Fremont ⑤
+1 206 547 2967
*pacinnpub.com*

If you've done your Seattle research via TV shows, you might recognize this unassuming pub from when Anthony Bourdain visited it on *Parts Unknown*. It wasn't a surprise to locals, who have long flocked here for the pub's phenomenal fish and chips. The clientele is always a mix of old timers and new Fremont residents, here for the first of many times.

## 29 ROCKCREEK SEAFOOD & SPIRITS

4300 Fremont
Avenue N
Fremont ⑤
+1 206 557 7532
*rockcreekseattle.com*

Go here with friends or family who love seafood as much as you, as it's a menu great for sharing and trying new things. If you can get there as soon as they open, the happy hour deals at the bar from 4-5.30 are excellent. Your only regret here will be that you don't have an unlimited appetite. Reservations recommended.

## 30 AQUA BY EL GAUCHO

2801 Alaskan Way
Pier 70
Belltown ①
+1 206 956 9171
*aquabyelgaucho.com*

High-quality seafood, service and a spectacular view is what you can expect at AQUA. It is a part of the El Gaucho family of high-end restaurants in the Seattle area, with a reputation for being a place people celebrate the most special occasions.

29. ROCKCREEK SEAFOOD & SPIRITS

# 5 delicious **BAKERIES**

---

### 31 **MACRINA BAKERY & CAFE**

2408 1st Avenue
Belltown ①
+1 206 448 4032
*macrinabakery.com*

Even if you don't make it to the Macrina Cafe, you'll likely have their bread at some point during your visit to Seattle as it's commonly sourced by local restaurants. Their Belltown Cafe is a great place to start your day with a bialy egg sandwich, or pick up a baguette and pastries for a picnic nearby at the Olympic Sculpture Garden nearby.

31 MACRINA BAKERY & CAFE

**32 BAKERY NOUVEAU**

137 15th Avenue E
Capitol Hill ③
+1 206 858 6957
*bakerynouveau.com*

The display cases at Bakery Nouveau show off so many pastries, cakes and breads that it can be a bit overwhelming to decide what you want to order. The breakfast pastries are probably their most popular offerings, but the cakes and tarts make great contributions to dinner parties.

**33 THE FLOUR BOX**

5520 Rainier
Avenue S
Hillman City ⑨
*theflourboxseattle.com*

The Flour Box specializes in filled brioche donuts and equally well-crafted coffee drinks. This petite bakery has a charming patio space. They are only open four days a week and regularly sell out of donuts by noon. Donut flavors change with the season, so we recommend coming back.

**34 UMAMI KUSHI**

9099 Seward Park
Avenue S
Dunlap ⑨
+1 206 723 1887
*umamikushi.com*

Umami Kushi is known around Seattle for two very different baked goods. Their top-notch beignets can be found at a few local restaurants and establishments. Their Japanese Okazu Pan, small grab-and-go breads with a savory filling, are phenomenal. Fillings include curry beef (the classic), lentil (vegan friendly) or even salmon, bacon and potato.

**35 NIELSEN'S PASTRIES**

520 2nd Avenue W
Lower Queen Anne ①
+1 206 282 3004
*nielsenspastries.com*

Nielsen's Pastries has been satisfying Seattle's sweet tooth since 1965. While purchased by new owners in 2017, the Danish pastry tradition lives on strongly here and they still use the original owner's recipes.

# 5 IMMIGRANT-RUN
## *restaurants*

---

### 36 CAFE TURKO
750 N 34th St
Fremont ⑤
+1 206 284 9954
*cafeturko.com*

Owners Gencer and Süreyya Gökeri expanded beyond their first business of Istanbul Imports to open Cafe Turko in 2012. Come here for dinner the next time you want to travel to the other side of the world without leaving Seattle. The homemade *ayran* is great on a hot day and the menu contains all halal and zabiha products. Their food works great for catering as well.

### 37 PHNOM PENH NOODLE HOUSE
913 S Jackson St
International
District ③
+1 206 785 6936
*phnompenhnoodle house.com*

We can't do the Phnom Penh owners' family story justice in this blurb, so be sure to check it out on their website before you visit this wonderful Cambodian restaurant. Their clean and modern space in the International District re-opened a few years ago with a slimmer menu, but favorites like *Samlaw Machou* soup and all the noodles you could wish for are still available.

36 **CAFE TURKO**

## 38 MAMA SAMBUSA KITCHEN

8319 Wabash
Avenue S
Dunlap ⑨
+1 206 457 9551
*mamasambusa
kitchen.com*

Founder Marian Ahmed emigrated from Somalia in 1996, opening Mama Sambusa in 2002 and bringing the restaurant to Seattle in 2009. She is proud to showcase her culture at Mama Sambusa and still makes the *sambusas* herself, which she recommends you have with the mama sauce. The menu is entirely halal.

## 39 POLISH HOME ASSOCIATION FRIDAY NIGHT DINNERS

1714 18th Avenue
Capitol Hill ③
+1 206 322 3020
*polishhome.org/
friday-dinner*

The Polish Home Association was established in 1918 as a place for people of Polish nationality and descent to come together for celebrations, festivals, meals, meetings and cultural exploration. Their Friday Night dinners are open to the public, guests just have to pay a nominal fee to become a member for the evening. Come hungry, but check the website as the kitchen occasionally closes down in summers!

## 40 ANNAPURNA CAFE

1833 Broadway
Avenue
Capitol Hill ③
+1 206 320 7770
*annapurnacafe.com*

Despite this restaurant being in a cozy basement, sometimes if the wind moves the right direction you can smell the mouthwatering Nepalese, Indian and Tibetan spices from blocks away. The food is reasonably priced, cooked perfectly and delivered by friendly staff. Owner Roshita Shrestha cooked her native Nepalese food overseas before bringing it to Seattle.

# *5 spots*

# FIT-FOR-FOODIES

41 **SPINASSE**
   **1531 14th Avenue**
   **Capitol Hill** ③
   **+1 206 251 7673**
   *spinasse.com*

People who love Spinasse LOVE Spinasse. Like the they-won't-stop-talking-about-it (or going there) type-of-love. But it's easy to understand why, as their delicate and carefully crafted pastas will be the highlight of your evening. Better yet, get the menu *degustazione* so you can try every *antipasto*, *primo* and *secondo* on the menu, family style.

42 **HOMER**
   **3013 Beacon**
   **Avenue S**
   **North Beacon Hill** ⑨
   **+1 206 785 6099**
   *restauranthomer.com*

This Beacon Hill restaurant serves Mediterranean and Middle Eastern-inspired cuisine, with dashes of the Pacific Northwest in seasonal offerings. Everything is prepared on the premises, and the menu is built for sharing. The Family Feast is their version of a tasting menu and at just 50 dollars/person, it won't break the bank.

## 43 EDEN HILL

**2209 Queen Anne Avenue N**
**Queen Anne** ④
**+1 206 708 6836**
*edenhillrestaurant.com*

Chef Maximillian Petty's Upper Queen Anne restaurant is an intimate, trendy spot offering inventive cuisine that is popular with foodies. It's a great special occasion restaurant and has a well-curated wine list. They focus on local, seasonal ingredients for their dishes that change sometimes daily. They have one of the must-do tasting menus in Seattle.

## 44 LARK

**952 E Seneca St**
**Capitol Hill** ③
**+1 206 323 5275**
*larkseattle.com*

This Capitol Hill landmark has been in operation for 20 years, though their beautiful space is just half as old. They offer a four-course dinner menu where you choose each course from a few options. Offerings change monthly and feature local produce, meats and cheeses. Wine pairings are available or you can bring in your own bottle, as long as it's not currently on the wine list.

## 45 DUMPLINGS OF FURY

**4302 SW Oregon St**
**The Junction** ⑧
**+1 206 257 0695**
*dumplingsoffury.com*

Dumplings of Fury is our pick for takeout or delivery fit for foodies. Their West Seattle location is a very casual, countertop service spot, but there is nothing casual about the care and attention given to the food on their menu. The shrimp and pork wontons, any of the *baos* and the spicy green beans are all a must-try. Enjoy these fine eats from the comfort of your own home, or take them for a picnic at nearby Alki Beach.

# 5 **WARM MEALS**
## *for a cold night*

---

46 **RADIATOR WHISKEY**
   **94 Pike St, #30**
   **Downtown** ②
   **+1 206 467 4268**
   *radiatorwhiskey.com*

Located one story above the hubbub of Pike Place market, this place is (surprise!) focused on whiskey and meat. Whether you like savory, slow cooked briskets or salty, fried pork shanks, meat lovers will enjoy themselves thoroughly. The smoked maple old fashioned goes well with just about everything on the menu. Reservations are recommended, especially in summer.

46 **RADIATOR WHISKEY**

## 47 LIL RED TAKEOUT AND CATERING

4225 Rainier
Avenue S
Columbia City ⑨
+1 206 760 2931
lilredtakeout.com

Their tagline is 'Jamaican BBQ & soul cuisine' and they are not kidding about the soul part. You really can't go wrong with any choice on this menu and it will warm your soul to eat it. The eat-in atmosphere is very casual but the staff are so friendly it's worth eating in just to chat a bit with them.

## 48 VIENGTHONG LAO RESTAURANT

2820 Martin Luther
King Jr Way S
Mt. Baker ⑨
+1 206 725 3884

This restaurant is in a small strip mall in the Mount Baker neighborhood and flies under the radar for Seattleites in other neighborhoods. But it stands out for those who know it as an authentic offering of Laotian food not found in many other places. You won't regret any order off their specials menu, or any of the soups.

## 49 CAFE MUNIR

2408 NW 80th St
Ballard ⑤
+1 206 472 4150

This unassuming yet casually elegant Lebanese restaurant in North Ballard has a small dining room that gets quite full at dinner time. You'll need to call to make a reservation or face a bit of a wait during the busiest times. The *mezze* options are great for sharing, as are the kabobs.

## 50 JERK SHACK

1133 24th Avenue
Central District ③
+1 206 441 7817
jerkshackseattle.com

Is there anything quite so belly-warming as jerk chicken? Quite a bit of local attention has been paid to this Caribbean restaurant, and for good reason. Chef Trey Lamont's Jamaican heritage inspires much of the menu. The plates are a great place to start on your first visit, don't miss out on the cocktail menu either.

# 5 *great* VEGETARIAN & VEGAN *eats*

51 **BA BAR GREEN**
   **500 Terry Avenue N**
   **South Lake Union** ①
   **+1 206 588 1022**
   *babargreen.com*

Ba Bar Green is the newly opened offshoot of the Monsoon and Ba Bar restaurant family. This vegan East Asian takeout window is perfect for a sunny day when you might want to sit outside at nearby Lake Union Park. For those new to or experimenting with vegan food, don't miss the *chorizo bánh mì*, you definitely won't miss the meat.

52 **CAFE FLORA**
   **2901 E Madison St**
   **Madison Valley** ③
   **+1 206 325 9100**
   *cafeflora.com*

Cafe Flora has been one of the pillars of the Seattle vegetarian restaurant scene for 30 years, and for good reason. Their cozy and colorful dining room in Madison Valley matches their lovingly crafted breakfast, lunch and dinner menus. A majority of menu items are or can be made vegan and even those in your party who aren't vegetarian will find something to love.

## 53 PLUM BISTRO

1429 12th Avenue
Capitol Hill ③
+1 206 838 5333
plumbistro.com

Chef Makini Howell was recognized in 2019 by *The New York Times* as one of sixteen Black chefs changing food in America. The Plum Bistro industrial-chic Capitol Hill space is usually full on weekends, especially for brunch, where you can't miss the Chick'n & Waffles, made of fried seitan. Reservations are available and recommended.

## 54 CHUMINH TOFU

1043 S Jackson St
International
District ③
+1 206 723 6095
chuminhtofu.com

This International District restaurant serves vegan Vietnamese dishes, with ample takeout options. The *bánh mìs* are particularly good and they operate an all-day buffet for those who want to see everything available to them. The owner, Thanh-Nga Nguyễn, serves free meals every Sunday to neighbors in need alongside volunteers who call themselves 'the egg rolls.'

## 55 THE WAYWARD VEGAN

801 NE 65th St,
Suite C
Roosevelt ⑥
+1 206 524 0204
waywardvegan
cafe.com

Think diner food, vegan style. The Wayward Vegan in Roosevelt is open every day, with breakfast served until 3.30 pm. Their expansive menu with lots of classic diner offerings (BBQ burgers, buffalo drumsticks, omelets galore) means you'll find whatever you're looking for. It's the perfect spot for a casual lunch before or after a walk around Green Lake.

# 5 locally loved
# QUICK EATS

---

### 56 MAMMOTH

5239 Ballard
Avenue NW
Ballard ⑤
+1 206 946 1065
*mammothseattle.com*

These sandwiches are so much more than a standard deli experience. While Mammoth's usual premise undergoes ongoing construction, they're operating out of their sister restaurant, Bitterroot BBQ. The relationship is undeniable, the attention paid to the ingredients in these sammies is noticeable. Get anything with their homemade ranch sauce.

### 57 TACO TIME NW

2212 N 45th St
Wallingford ⑤
+1 206 547 7217
*tacotimenw.com*

Want food that's incredibly fast but locally sourced and from a family-owned chain? Head to one of Taco Time NW's many Western Washington locations. It's a great pit stop while you're on a day trip outside the city, or if you're stretched for time between activities in town. The fish tacos are great and there are plenty of options for kids on the menu, too.

### 58 BISCUIT BITCH

2303 3rd Avenue
Belltown ①
+1 206 728 2219
*biscuitbitch.com*

Perhaps not a spot to bring the youngest family members, depending on your comfort level with salty language. Both the sausage gravy and the gluten-free and vegetarian mushroom gravy are delicious.

## 59  UN BIEN

6226 Seaview
Avenue NW
Ballard ⑤
+1 206 420 7545
unbienseattle.com

With two locations in Ballard, Un Bien's sandwiches are basically designed to be taken for a picnic at Golden Gardens or Gas Works Park. You can't go wrong with any of the Caribbean restaurant's sandwiches (all on Macrina baked bread), but the entrees are worth experimenting with as well. Any dish with the caramelized onions is a must-try.

## 60  DICK'S DRIVE-IN

500 Queen Anne
Avenue N
Lower Queen Anne ①
+1 206 285 5155
ddir.com

Dick's is *the* Seattle fast food burger. The Queen Anne location is particularly convenient to Seattle Center, and 'the special' (a single patty) will only set you back 3,20 dollars. When is the last time you had a good fast food burger for under 5 dollars? Much less a double patty burger, fries and a root beer float for under 10 dollars? Saving money never tasted so good.

# 5 spots for Seattle
# DONUTS

---

61 **TOP POT DOUGHNUTS**
2124 5th Avenue
Belltown ①
+1 206 728 1966
*toppotdoughnuts.com*

Okay, Top Pot donuts aren't exactly hidden in Seattle, but they are excellent. Their flagship store in Belltown is well worth a visit (President Obama has even visited) and has ample seating to linger over your sweet treat. Try the classic combination of a latte and a glazed old fashioned.

62 **KING DONUTS**
7820 Rainier
Avenue S
Rainier Valley ⑨
+1 206 721 3103
*kingdonutsseattle.com*

King Donuts in Rainier Valley just moved to a new location, which is great for them but means you'll miss out on the opportunity to do your laundry at the same time. (The business used to be at a location that housed a teriyaki shop and laundromat.) Never fear, you'll be enjoying their buttermilk and raised donuts too much to miss the former quirks.

63 **MIGHTY-O DONUTS**
2110 N 55th St
Green Lake ⑤
+1 206 547 5431
*mightyo.com*

Vegans, and their companions, will be delighted with the wide variety of classic donut options at Mighty O's. From simple standards like cinnamon & sugar or glazed to slightly more inventive combinations like 'the grasshopper'.

64 **DOUGH JOY**

4310 SW Oregon St
The Junction ⑧
+1 206 453 5658
*doughjoydonuts.com*

Dough Joy represents the other side of the donut-wave, catering also to vegans, but to those with more experimental palates. Flavors like grapefruit cherry shortbread and rose cardamom will tempt your tastebuds while you likely wait in line on a weekend morning. The West Seattle location is attached to their charming plant area, 'Botanic! at the Disco'.

65 **GOOD DAY DONUTS**

9823 15th Avenue SW
White Center ⑧
+1 206 503 2898
*gooddaydonuts.com*

White Center isn't technically in Seattle, it's just south of West Seattle, but it's worth a visit for many dining spots, especially Good Day Donuts. The special fritter on Friday is always a treat, though some may prefer the French Crullers on Saturday. They also offer several savory breakfast and lunch sandwiches, with at least one or two vegan options.

61 TOP POT DOUGHNUTS

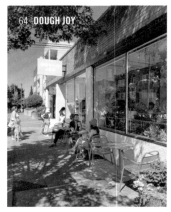
64 DOUGH JOY

# 5 places to satisfy your
# SWEET TOOTH

---

66 **HUSKY DELI & ICE CREAM**

4721 California
Avenue SW
The Junction ⑧
+1 206 937 2810
*huskydeli.com*

Husky Deli & Ice Cream was established in 1932, and the storefront doesn't seem to have changed too much in that 90 years (in a good way!). With more than 40 flavors of homemade ice cream, you can guarantee your sweet tooth will be satisfied. Better yet, if you need something savory to go with that, be it dry goods or a great sandwich, you can also find it there.

67 **THEO CHOCOLATE**

3400 Phinney
Avenue N
Fremont ⑤
+1 206 632 5100
*theochocolate.com*

While Theo Chocolate recently announced they'll be discontinuing much of their Seattle-based chocolate production, we hope the smell of cocoa will linger for a long time around their Fremont facility. Their headquarters, flagship store and confectionery shop will remain in place and are still very worth a stop to satisfy your sweet tooth while you're in the neighborhood.

## 68 MOLLY MOON'S HOMEMADE ICE CREAM

917 E Pine St
Capitol Hill ③
+1 206 294 4389
mollymoon.com

The Molly Moon's location in Capitol Hill can have a line at any time of day, even in the dead of winter. Their classic flavors are great, but it's worth getting a few scoops to try one of the seasonal offerings at the same time. The local chain focuses on sustainability and community, sourcing 90% of their ingredients in the PNW and returning 10% of their profits to nonprofits.

## 69 CREAMY CONE CAFE

9433 Rainier
Avenue S
Rainier Beach ⑨
+1425 243 7983

This small, woman-owned ice-cream shop is one of several businesses worth visiting in the southernmost end of Seattle. The prices are truly reasonable, so you can splurge on several scoops and enjoy them at one of the nearby waterfront access points, like Chinook Beach Park or Be'er Sheva Park.

## 70 HELLO ROBIN

522 19th Avenue E
Capitol Hill ③
+1 206 735 7970
hellorobincookies.com

Hello Robin's 'best cookie in Seattle' claim is a bold one – but it's held up so far. The cookies are particularly enjoyable when sandwiched around a scoop of Molly Moon's ice cream. The owners of the two shops are friends (and aren't we all lucky for that?). Speaking of great partnerships, the Mackles'more is a s'more cookie with a chunk of Theo chocolate. Yum.

## 5 meals to
# START YOUR DAY

---

71 **ARTHUR'S**
2311 California
Avenue SW
North Admiral ⑧
+1 206 829 8235
*arthursseattle.com*

A classic and stylish all-day cafe, Arthur's offers great breakfast and lunch options, with some evening hours on weekends. The cafe is filled to the brim with plants, you'll feel like you're in a trendy friend's apartment. The ricotta pancakes and Arthur's brunch bowl will be hard to decide between. The delicious house-smoked trout is a must try.

71 ARTHUR'S

## 72 BRYANT CORNER CAFE

3118 NE 65th St
Ravenna ⑥
+1 206 525 1034
*thebryantcorner
cafe.com*

This bakery and cafe is a Northeast Seattle locals' favorite. Breakfast is served all day, so you can enjoy the meal whenever your day happens to start. They offer several ways to enjoy their homemade Dungeness crab cakes, a true northwest treat. This place is definitely family friendly.

## 73 FAT'S CHICKEN AND WAFFLES

2726 E Cherry St
Central District ③
+1 206 602 6863
*fatschickenand
waffles.com*

It wouldn't be a mistake to head to Fat's as soon as you wake up on a Saturday or Sunday, as the wait can be astronomical later in the morning for brunch. Everyone's entitled to their own choices, but there's a reason this place is named for chicken and waffles.

## 74 THE COUPE & FLUTE

3015 Beacon
Avenue S
North Beacon Hill ⑨

If you've searched all your life for somewhere with a 'champagne tavern' vibe, look no further. The Coupe & Flute recently opened on Beacon Hill and offers a great weekend brunch along with a small plates-focused dinner menu, all designed to pair well with bubbly.

## 75 HARBOR CITY

707 S King St
International
District ③
+1 206 621 2228
*harborcityseattle.com*

Dim Sum options abound in the International District, but a great starting point for visitors is Harbor City. They serve all the traditional Chinese dim sum menu items in a relaxed environment. If it's your first dim sum experience, come hungry and not in a rush, ideally in a group so you can try as many dishes as your heart desires.

# 5 FOOD TRUCKS
## *worth finding*

---

**76 EL CAMION**
Location varies
*elcamionseattle.com*

The El Camion food trucks are a Seattle institution. Serving some of the city's best Mexican food, the only thing patrons can't agree on is what menu item is best. Whatever you're craving, be it tacos, burritos, *chilaquiles* or *gorditas*, you'll find something to like at El Camion. They just recently launched online ordering for all their food truck locations.

**77 FALAFEL SALAM**
Location varies
*falafelsalam.com*

This Middle Eastern food truck bounces around between farmers markets and breweries, though they also have a brick-and-mortar location in West Seattle if your schedules don't quite line up. 'The hesitator' is a great choice for those who have trouble making decisions. Both salad options are great, though the purple really pops on your plate.

## 78 OFF THE REZ

Location varies
*offthereztruck.com/
locationsschedule*

Seattle's first Native food truck also has a cafe on the University of Washington campus and a catering business. All the tacos are served on traditional frybread, made with a recipe from the Blackfeet tribal heritage of one of the owners. The truck can often be found at breweries on the weekends; check their page for the latest schedule.

## 79 TAT'S DELICATESSEN

Location varies
+1 206 373 1657
*tatsdeli.com/tats-truck*

Plan ahead for a visit to Tat's and come (very) hungry. The servings are on the large side and many a nap has been taken after finishing one of their sandwiches for lunch. The hot subs are particularly great, though the hoagies also meet a void in the Seattle lunch scene that was acutely felt by East Coast transplants.

## 80 LULA SALADS

Location varies
+1 206 866 0405
*lulasalads.com*

When Lula parks downtown on a week-day, office workers line up starting just after 11 am. Their options are narrow, but all great. More importantly, in an age when it feels impossible to get a high quality, interesting salad for under 15 dollars, their options all list under 10 dollars. They also have a brick-and-mortar location in Wallingford.

# 5 Seattle RESTAURANT INSTITUTIONS

81 **FARESTART GUEST CHEF NIGHTS & CAFE**
700 Virginia St
South Lake Union
+1 206 267 7601
*farestart.org*

FareStart is a local nonprofit organization dedicated to transforming lives through food. They offer job training programs that integrate seamlessly with their brick-and-mortar restaurant and cafes. Keep an eye on their calendar for the return of Guest Chef Nights, where program participants cook under the direction of well-known local chefs.

82 **MESKEL**
2605 E Cherry St
Central District ③
+1 206 860 1724
*meskelethiopian.com*

Meskel has been serving great Ethiopian food to Seattleites for over 25 years. Seattle is home to one of the largest groups of Ethiopian immigrants in the United States, and this restaurant is a great place to go to try this food for the first time (or for the fiftieth!).

83 **EZELL'S FAMOUS CHICKEN**
501 23rd Avenue
Central District ③
+1 206 324 4141
*ezellschicken.com*

If you're craving fried chicken, there are several great options in Seattle, but none quite so iconic as Ezell's. They opened in 1984 and have catered many special events over the years, but none perhaps so famous as Oprah's birthday in 1990. The Central District location is the original.

## 84 LINDA'S TAVERN

**707 E Pine St**
**Capitol Hill** ③
**+1 206 325 1220**
*lindastavern.com*

Most people who live in Seattle have been to Linda's at least once. Okay maybe that's an unfounded statement, but it certainly is a local standby. Can't decide where to go for brunch? Let's go to Linda's. Grabbing a drink with friends before a Capitol Hill dinner reservation? Linda's! It's always lively and the back patio is packed on a nice day.

## 85 SALTY'S ON ALKI

**1936 Harbor**
**Avenue SW**
**West Seattle** ⑧
**+1 206 937 1600**
*saltys.com/seattle*

Salty's is a traditional seafood restaurant with killer views of the Seattle Skyline and Elliott Bay. Sit outside in the summertime to soak in the sea air while you enjoy a glass of Washington wine and one of their classic seafood entrees. They're also well-known for their weekend brunch, especially the seafood scramble. Reservations recommended.

85 SALTY'S ON ALKI

STARBUCKS RESERVE ROASTERY

# 80 PLACES FOR A DRINK

---

5 top **COCKTAIL** spots —————— 66

5 great **FIRST DATE** drinks spots —————— 68

5 places to get your **CAFFEINE FIX** —————— 70

5 places to drink **LIKE A LOCAL** —————— 72

5 places for **SAMPLES GALORE** —————— 74

5 of the best **WINERY** tasting rooms —————— 76

5 great **BREWERIES** —————— 79

5 unique **SEATTLE BEERS** —————— 81

5 spots for **HAPPY HOUR** —————— 83

The 5 **COZIEST BARS** for cloudy weather —————— 85

5 places for drinks **WITH A VIEW** —————— 87

The 5 best **OUTDOOR** drinking spots —————— 90

5 spots with great **BAR GAMES** ———————— 94

5 bars with great **DRAG SHOWS** ———————— 96

5 bars to **SING YOUR HEART OUT** ———————— 98

5 great **LGBTQ+** bars ———————————— 100

# 5 top
# COCKTAIL *spots*

---

86 **THE NOOK**
**2206 California**
**Avenue SW, Suite A**
**North Admiral** ⑧
**+1 206 420 7414**
*thenookseattle.com*

Inside this small, cozy cocktail bar feels nothing like the modern building it is housed in in North Admiral. The bar gives off apothecary vibes with dozens of in-house made tinctures and syrups. One of the owners often staffs the bar and is happy to recommend one of her cocktails or another great one you should try at a different bar across town. Any negroni or mezcal cocktail will be spectacular.

87 **ZIG ZAG CAFE**
**1501 Western**
**Avenue, Suite 202**
**Downtown** ②
**+1 206 625 1146**
*zigzagseattle.com*

A book could be written on the history of Zig Zag Cafe (and it's worth googling to help you appreciate the storied history of this bar). Order 'the last word' to sip on while you read up on the role this bar and some of its famous bartenders played in the cocktail renaissance in America. The location seems to be right on top of Pike Place Market but you'll feel worlds away in their candle-lit retro space.

## 88 BATHTUB GIN & CO

**2205 2nd Avenue, #310**
**Belltown** ①
**+1 206 728 6069**
*bathtubginseattle.com*

In the past ten years we've kind of overdone the use of the word speakeasy to describe ordinary bars, but Bathtub Gin & Co is deserving of the label in the best way. Stroll up to the unassuming door (in the evenings it's more easily identified by the bouncer standing outside) and enjoy passing through time as you step inside this dim, multi-level emporium of great gin-based cocktails.

## 89 CANON

**928 12th Avenue**
**Capitol Hill** ③
*canonseattle.com*

For true cocktail aficionados, Canon will not be an unfamiliar name. But for those of us new to exploring the glory of these drinks, this bar is a must-visit in Seattle. Boasting "America's largest spirit collection" and incredibly knowledgeable bar staff, you can find whatever suits your fancy here. The "Canon's cannon" (their signature cocktail) is an excellent place to start your palate's adventures.

## 90 STAMPEDE COCKTAIL CLUB

**119 N 36th St**
**Fremont** ⑤
**+1 206 420 2792**
*stampedecocktail club.com*

Ready to take a break from the breweries that overwhelm the Ballard and Fremont neighborhoods? Head to Stampede Cocktail Club for inventive cocktails and a trendy setting with some nice street-side patio seating for good weather. They serve a few varieties of dumplings to help soak up their more alcohol-forward offerings. Also on the menu are several excellent N/A cocktails.

# 5 *great* **FIRST DATE**
## *drinks spots*

---

91 **LIBERTY**
   **517 15th Avenue E**
   **Capitol Hill** ③
   **+1 206 323 9898**
   *libertybarseattle.com*

Liberty is a tried-and-true date spot for Seattleites of all kinds. They have a great location on Capitol Hill, a casual environment that's usually full of other people on dates, and quality cocktail offerings. If you're feeling the vibe you can extend your stay and enjoy their sushi offerings. There's even a happy hour roll for just 7 dollars.

92 **BOTTLEHOUSE**
   **1416 34th Avenue**
   **Madrona** ③
   **+1 206 708 7164**
   *bottlehouseseattle.com*

This is the perfect place for someone who loves wine (or is just getting into wine and wants some guidance on what they like). They have a great daily happy hour from 3-6 pm as well as a late-night menu from 10 pm to close. The converted single-family home is tucked away in the upscale Madrona neighborhood. Order the charcuterie board and a new-to-you glass of wine (perhaps one that is on tap!) and enjoy the stylish interior and learning from the knowledgeable staff.

## 93 CORVUS AND COMPANY

**601 Broadway E**
**Capitol Hill** ③
**+1 206 420 8488**
*corvusandcompany.com*

Corvus & Co has the dim, chic interior of a bar that many folks think of when they're planning a romantic date night. Their enormous (and beautiful) bar inspires plenty of outstanding cocktails and their North Capitol Hill location is convenient to plenty of other bars, restaurants and activities for further enjoyment. They're currently hosting Big Dumpling Energy who serve Asian street food and shared plates.

## 94 TEKU TAVERN + CAFE

**552 Denny Way**
**South Lake Union** ①
**+1 206 466 1764**
*tekutavern.beer*

TeKu Tavern is named after the quintessential TeKu beer glass, designed in Italy to be a standardized glass that could offer maximum the user's enjoyment of beer. And there is certainly plenty of beer to go around at TeKu Tavern, with 56 beers, ciders, meads and wines on tap. This is a great place to take someone who likes to try new things, and you can even bring something new home from their bottle shop.

## 95 NEW LUCK TOY

**5905 California**
**Avenue SW**
**West Seattle** ⑧
*newlucktoy.bar*

This hidden away West Seattle gem is a favorite of just about everyone after their first visit. Despite the unassuming exterior, inside is hip, loud and always busy. They serve excellent (Americanized) Chinese food and great drinks, including several rotating slushies. The fried rice flavors are not-to-miss and whatever is on special that night is worth getting.

# 5 places to get your
# CAFFEINE FIX

---

**96 QUEEN MARY TEA ROOM**
**2912 NE 55th St**
**Ravenna** ⑥
**+1 206 527 2770**
*queenmarytea.com*

Queen Mary Tea Room is the oldest independently owned tea room in the United States, open since 1988. Stop by their nearby (half a block away) Tea Emporium for all your take-home tea needs, but visit the tea room for a truly special experience. Brunch and lunch offer traditional menus to select from while afternoon tea includes a variety of small bite options to accompany your pot of Queen Mary tea.

**97 MILSTEAD & CO.**
**754 N 34th St**
**Fremont** ⑤
**+1 206 659 4814**
*milsteadandco.com*

Milstead & Co. is the coffee aficionado's coffee spot in North Seattle. Their airy, industrial setup is a great spot to meet a colleague or friend before or after exploring Fremont. Their knowledgeable baristas are friendly and they source their coffee from a few different roasters to meet multiple palate preferences, including Stumptown, Intelligentsia, and Coava.

## 98 UPTOWN ESPRESSO

**3223 W McGraw St**
**Magnolia** ④
**+1 206 217 4463**
*uptownespresso.com*

Uptown Espresso is 'the home of the velvet foam' and an early entry into Seattle's coffee scene in the early 1980s. You can pair your latte with one of their all-day sandwich offerings at one of their five locations around the city. Their Pier 70 location is particularly convenient for caffeine-infusions before or after a walk through the Olympic Sculpture Garden.

## 99 COFFEEHOLIC HOUSE

**3700 S Hudson St**
**Columbia City** ⑨
**+1 206 722 3327**
*coffeeholichouse.com*

Coffeeholic House has been keeping its Columbia City neighbors buzzing since they opened in March 2020. They pride themselves in being Seattles' first Vietnamese coffee shop and offer a number of original caffeinated creations. The highlight, unsurprisingly, is their Vietnamese coffee which uses beans from Vietnam and is brewed traditionally with Phin filter drip methods.

## 100 STARBUCKS RESERVE ROASTERY

**1124 Pike St**
**Capitol Hill** ③
**+1 206 624 0173**
*starbucks.com/store-locator/store/1007342*

You can't really talk about coffee in Seattle without talking about Starbucks. While many tourists will end up trapped in the endless line at the Pike Place Market 'original' location, the better choice is to walk up towards Capitol Hill and admire the astonishingly large first-ever Starbucks Reserve Roastery. Sip on the rarest Starbucks blends from around the world while enjoying this high-design space.

# 5 *places to drink*
# LIKE A LOCAL

---

### 101 THE 5 POINT CAFE

415 Cedar St
Belltown ①
+1 206 448 9991
*the5pointcafe.com/
main-menu*

The neon sign in the window says 'We cheat tourists-n-drunks since 1929' – which doesn't feel particularly welcoming, but once you read the lengthy history of The 5 Point on their website, you'll be too intrigued not to venture in to see for yourself. One of the longest family-run spots in Seattle, you can stop in any time of day, as they're open 24 hours/day.

### 102 HATTIE'S HAT

5231 Ballard
Avenue NW
Ballard ⑤
+1 206 784 0175
*hatties-hat.com*

Brunch at Hattie's Hat is something of a right of passage for Seattle transplants as they adapt to the Seattle scene and get acquainted with local legends. Stepping inside feels like you've moved backwards in time. The giant bar looks like it hasn't changed in decades (it probably hasn't). The bloody marys are on point, the portions are hearty and the neon "cocktails" sign should be on your photo safari list.

## 103 WEDGWOOD ALE HOUSE & CAFE

**8515 35th Avenue NE**
**Wedgwood** ⑥
**+1 206 527 2676**
*wedgwoodalehouse.com*

No uppity big-city bar vibes to see here. Wedgwood Ale House has friendly staff and a rotating cast of regulars that make you feel like you're on an 80s sitcom set. There are three different parts of the business, including the main pub, speakeasy, and cafe (for family dining). This speakeasy hosts the pool table and the coziest winter vibe and it's even available for private rental.

## 104 SULLY'S SNOW GOOSE SALOON

**6119 Phinney**
**Avenue N**
**Phinney Ridge** ⑤

This tiny bar perched atop Phinney Ridge is quaintly decorated and cozy-as-all-get-out in the dark winter months with a fireplace patrons can sit close to. Many locally produced beers are available on tap, and you'll find plenty of regulars posted up to watch one Seattle sports game or another on the few TVs above the bar area.

## 105 TARGY'S TAVERN

**600 W Crockett St**
**Queen Anne** ④
**+1 206 352 8882**
*targysseattle.com*

Spend some time walking around Upper Queen Anne ahead of your visit to Targy's, and you'll be even more jolted by the casual, old school vibe of this bar. Founded in 1937, Targy's has a giant U-shaped bar around which all manner of locals, young and old, gather. Stop in for Bingo on Tuesdays or Trivia on Wednesdays.

## 5 places for
# SAMPLES GALORE

—————

### 106 SCHILLING CIDER HOUSE

**708 N 34th St**
**Fremont** ⑤
**+1 206 420 7088**
*schillingcider.com*

Washington State is the top producer of the United State's total apple crop. We're also a top producer of pears, sweet cherries and blueberries, so it's only fitting that you spend some time sampling ciders during your visit. Schilling is a great place to do this, with a convenient Fremont location (a break from all the nearby beer!) and more than 30 locally produced ciders on tap to sample.

### 107 OUNCES TAPROOM & BEER GARDEN

**3809 Delridge Way SW**
**West Seattle** ⑧
**+1 206 420 1837**
*ounceswestseattle.com*

Tucked just off the West Seattle Bridge in North Delridge, you aren't likely to just stumble upon this taproom. It's worth an intentional visit to sample their wide variety of Washington-made beers, ciders and wines. They've got a small indoor area but ample outdoor space, that's open to all ages. Their tap list is regularly updated online and they often have food trucks parked nearby on weekends.

## 108 CHUCK'S HOP SHOP

**5041 Wilson Avenue S**
**Seward Park** ⑨
**+ 1 206 485 2977**
*chuckshopshop.com*

All three Chuck's locations are worth visiting, but the Central District location is a good jumping off point to several other Central District restaurants to try before or after your visit. They regularly have 50 different beers and ciders on tap. To avoid being overwhelmed upon arrival, you can even view the live tap list for each location online ahead of time, or just ask the friendly counter staff for a recommendation.

## 109 RIDGEWOOD BOTTLE & TAP

**316 N 67th St**
**Phinney Ridge** ⑤
**+1 206 453 4838**
*ridgewoodbottle andtap.com*

Located in Phinney Ridge, this bottle & taphouse is usually full of nearby residents. You'll be sure to find a good local beverage to enjoy from their 30 taps, which mostly focus on beer but include other options as well. They encourage you to bring nearby local food in to enjoy (we'd recommend Red Mill Burgers or Wing Dome).

## 110 SODO URBANWORKS

**3931 1st Avenue, Suite 2236**
**SoDo** ⑨
*sodo-urbanworks.com*

The only thing working against this great collaboratively managed space is its location, deep in the SoDo neighborhood that's hard to get to without a car. We recommend splurging on a ride share so you can enjoy more than one tasting at one of the many wineries housed in this space. Nine Hats Wines and Sleight of Hand Cellars are standouts. Those not interested in wine can head to San Juan Seltzer's tasting room.

# 5 of the best
# **WINERY** *tasting rooms*

111 **TINTE CELLARS**
**5951 Airport Way S**
**Georgetown** ⑨
**+1 206 829 9941**
*tintecellars.com*

Friendly staff and a plethora of unique events (plus weekly Thursday happy hour specials) anchor the new urban industrial tasting room for this family-owned winery. The tasting flight changes monthly but glass pours of any favorites are always available. Their Malbec is particularly enjoyable on a damp winter night.

112 **BROWNE FAMILY VINEYARDS TASTING ROOM**
**413 1st Avenue S**
**Pioneer Square** ②
**+1 206 887 9463**
*brownefamily vineyards.com*

As the name implies, this is a family-owned winery that produces wine in Walla Walla, the heart of wine country in eastern Washington. Their Pioneer Square tasting room is a stylish space, perfectly paired with the Bordeaux reds and full body white wines that you'll be tasting. Reservations are strongly encouraged, as space is limited here.

## 113 DELILLE CELLARS

14300 NE 145th St
Suite 101
Woodinville
+1 425 489 0544
*delillecellars.com*

Get out of the city and into nearby Woodinville, Seattle's closest 'wine country'. There are dozens of tasting rooms to choose from in the area, but DeLille Cellars stands out as both some of the best Bordeaux-inspired wine in the area, but also one of the harder reservations to get, so plan ahead. Their restaurant offers a great happy hour, a sneaky way to taste and snack at the same time.

## 114 THE PRINCESS & BEAR

309 S Cloverdale St,
Suite A1
South Park ⑨
+1 206 323 4757
*theprincessand thebear.com*

Truly a hidden secret, Princess & Bear wines is a charming tasting room located in an industrial park in Seattle's South Park neighborhood. The owners import wines for tasting exclusively from the Languedoc-Roussillon region of France. A tasting here offers a wonderful change up from Washington-wine focused tasting rooms, and the staff are wonderfully educational.

## 115 ELSOM CELLARS

2960 4th Avenue S,
Suite 114
SoDo ⑨
+1 425 298 3082
*elsomcellars.com*

Elsom boasts that their wines are Seattle-made and Washington-grown, how much more local can you get? Their women-led winery focuses on small-batch wines, and their farmhouse-inspired tasting room in SoDo is a great respite from the urban industrial surroundings. They have a big focus on community through their Community Label wines, that give a portion of profits back to local nonprofits.

117 STOUP

# 5 great
# BREWERIES

---

### 116 REUBEN'S BREWS

**5010 14th
Avenue NW
Ballard** ⑤
**+1 206 784 2859**
*reubensbrews.com*

Whether you're at a restaurant, a bar, a tap room or a grocery store, you're pretty likely to come across a Reuben's Brews offering. The Taproom in Ballard is always overflowing with people, but it's still worth a visit to try a beer fresh from the brewing facilities behind the cash register. Their seasonal offerings are excellent, but the Crikey IPA and Pilsner are classics.

### 117 STOUP

**1108 NW 52nd St
Ballard** ⑤
**+1 206 457 5524**
*stoupbrewing.com*

Stoup Brewing's space has it all, a spacious outdoor area for days without rain, an upstairs annex with TVs for sports watchers, and an industrial indoor tasting area that's full pretty much every hour of every day. Their wide range of beers are all pretty great, but the Mosaic Pale Ale, Citra IPA and NW Red are all classics. They have a food truck on the premises every day of the week.

## 118 HOLY MOUNTAIN BREWING COMPANY

**1421 Elliott Avenue W**
**Interbay** ④
**+1 206 457 5279**
*holymountain brewing.com*

Holy Mountain boasts of being the original oak and barrel-focused brewery in Seattle. Their offerings are anything and everything in between funky (saisons!), deep and dank (bourbon barrel aged) or crisp and classic (lagers and pale ales). It's worth doing a tasting (or two) here to appreciate the wide variety of creative brews. Make Holy Mountain your destination at the end of the Elliott Bay Park walk!

## 119 METIER BREWING COMPANY TAPROOM

**2616 E Cherry St**
**Central District** ③
**+1 425 415 8466**
*metierbrewing.com*

Metier Brewing Company is a Black-owned craft brewery dedicated to great beer and building community. Their taproom in the Central District boasts several exclusive beers and food available from Umami Kushi. The barrel aged amber rye beer is a perfect fall or winter brew, while their Belgian wit is exactly what you want to drink on a patio on a sunny summer day.

## 120 THE GOOD SOCIETY BREWERY & PUBLIC HOUSE

**2701 California Avenue SW, Unit A**
**North Admiral** ⑧
**+1 206 420 3528**
*goodsocietybeer.com*

Good Society is a relatively small brewery compared to some of the others on this list, but their airy and friendly spot in West Seattle is well worth a visit. Order a tasting and be sure not to miss their award winning grissette, First to Fall. Your other options are widely varied, from a number of IPA varieties to a delicious *Schwarzbier* or a summery favorite, Pool Party.

# 5 unique
# SEATTLE BEERS

---

### 121 MANNY'S
AT: GEORGETOWN
BREWING CO.
**5200 Denver
Avenue S
Georgetown** ⑨
**+1 206 766 8055**
*georgetownbeer.com*

While there aren't reliable statistics on the most commonly listed craft beers on draft lists at restaurants and bars around the city, Manny's would likely be at the top of that list. It is a refreshing, flavorful pale ale that's not to be missed. You can't buy it in stores, so you'll have to order it out, which is great because it's definitely a beer made for being enjoyed on draft.

### 122 RAINIER
AT: MOST BARS
*rainierbeer.com*

Did you even go to Seattle if you didn't have a Rainier? While this brew is no longer produced in Washington (nor is it locally owned), ordering a Rainier at a dive bar, concert or sporting event is a classic PNW rite of passage. The iconic R logo will greet you as you drive northward into Seattle on the I-5 and you should definitely loop up the Rainier advertising campaigns of the 80s for a laugh.

### 123 AFRICAN AMBER

AT: MAC & JACK'S
BREWERY
**17825 NE 65th St**
**Redmond**
**+1 425 558 9697**
*macandjacks.com*

This dry-hopped amber ale is malty with a mild hop-spiced punch. The color and flavor profile make it a great fall beer to pair with cooler weather and (American) football season. You can find it on tap at many bars and restaurants around the city and it's also available for purchase in cans in local grocery stores. They have a taproom open daily in Redmond and free brewery tours on Saturdays.

### 124 FREMONT LUSH IPA

AT: FREMONT BREWING
**1050 N 34th St**
**Fremont** ⑤
**+1 206 420 2407**
*fremontbrewing.com*

We couldn't write a list about Seattle beers without including a Northwest IPA. This hoppy IPA is regularly winning national beer awards and can be found in almost any grocery store around the city. The can art featuring some classic NW hops, will help you identify this plant. Just on the other side of the Cascade Mountains sits Yakima Valley, home to the vast majority of the United States' hops crop.

### 125 AMERICAN-STYLE PILS

AT: CLOUDBURST
**5456 Shilshole**
**Avenue NW**
**Ballard** ⑤
*cloudburstbrew.com*

Cloudburst Brewing produces such dependably delicious beers that this author will pretty much order any beer of theirs at a bar without asking about it. Their American-style Pils keeps winning World Beer Cup awards, so be sure to seek that out, but their wide array of IPAs is also great. Their half pint-sized tasting room near Pike Place is very small, so head to their Ballard location for more room to spread out.

# 5 spots for
# HAPPY HOUR

---

### 126 SOME RANDOM BAR
**2604 1st Avenue**
**Belltown** ①
*somerandombar.com*

The owners and staff at Some Random Bar are friendly and funny, which you can sense through their menu designating 'no crap on tap' and signs around the bar mocking the 'Seattle freeze.' Aside from the nice service, though, you should come here for the crab nachos. Yes, crab meat on nachos sounds different, but it is spectacular. Enjoy deals on food and drinks at their great happy hour.

### 127 ALIBI ROOM
**85 Pike St, #410**
**Downtown** ②
**+1 206 623 3180**
*thealibiroom.com*

The entrance to Alibi Room's Pike Place location is just across from the infamous Seattle gum wall. If you still have an appetite after checking out that odd landmark, pop in here for their solid happy hour deals offered from opening until 4 pm every day. Draft beers, well drinks and select wines are all 5 dollars or less.

## 128 VON'S 1000 SPIRITS

**1225 1st Avenue**
**Downtown** ②
**+1 206 621 8667**
*vons1000spirits.com*

Von's is a great place for food and drinks in downtown Seattle that won't break the bank, especially at happy hour. While the days of the 3-dollar Manhattan are sadly behind us, the 6-dollar Scratch Martini is still pretty hard to beat anywhere in the city. Enjoy your discounted drink with one of their homemade sourdough pizzas or other locally inspired discounted appetizers.

## 129 BAKER'S

**6408 32nd**
**Avenue NW**
**Sunset Hill** ⑤
**+1 206 353 1804**
*bakersseattle.com*

Baker's is a small restaurant and bar tucked up in Sunset Hill that would make a great afternoon destination after a visit to the Ballard Locks (which are just a half a mile south). Their happy hour is available Sunday-Thursday and all day on Mondays. It includes rotating apertifs, wines and fun snacks to help you soak that all up. Their outdoor seating area is particularly lovely on a sunny afternoon.

## 130 THE ATHENIAN SEAFOOD RESTAURANT AND BAR

**1517 Pike Place**
**Downtown** ②
**+1 206 624 7166**
*athenianseattle.com*

If you find yourself near Pike Place in the afternoon and need some budget-friendly food and drink, pop into The Athenian in Pike Place. Their lounge (which is 21+) has a wide variety of 5-to-6-dollar food and drink options, including a wide array of local craft beers, sliders, tacos and seafood snacks. Check their website for details on available days and times.

# The 5 COZIEST BARS
## for cloudy weather

---

### 131 DAMN THE WEATHER
**116 1st Avenue S**
**Pioneer Square** ②
**+1 206 946 1283**
*damntheweather.com*

Where else would you go when it's damp and dreary than a bar explicitly dedicated to acknowledging Seattle's rough off season. Damn the Weather offers creative cocktails, local beers and wines, along with chic PNW shareable plates. Their cozy, brick-walled interior usually has plenty of candles lit in the dark hours to enhance the *hygge* vibe in the dark months.

### 132 QUINN'S PUB
**1001 E Pike St**
**Capitol Hill** ③
**+1 206 325 7711**
*quinnspubseattle.com*

Quinn's is a Seattle institution in the heart of Capitol Hill. They serve updated classics in a modern pub setting that is cozy and bustling most hours of the day. Their happy hour is worth checking out for the half-off draft beers or the 5-dollar margarita, especially right when they open when you're more likely to get a seat.

## 133 BEVERIDGE PLACE PUB

**6413 California Avenue SW**
**West Seattle** ⑧
**+1 206 932 9906**
*beveridgeplacepub.com*

Beveridge Place Pub has two sections, one made for dim and dreary afternoons or evenings when you want to enjoy a great pint in a cozy, British pub-vibe atmosphere. The other half of the pub hosts several bar games (darts, shuffleboard, etc.) and TVs for enjoying whatever sporting event is on. They also have ample outdoor seating for the nicer months and an expansive beer list to suit whatever you fancy.

## 134 LOTTIE'S LOUNGE

**4900 Rainier Avenue S**
**Columbia City** ⑨
**+1 206 725 0519**
*lottieslounge.com*

This casual and cozy bar calls itself 'Columbia City's living room since 1998.' It's a small, intimate space that's best for small parties. Their food menu is narrow (just tacos and nachos) but there's a wide selection of cocktails. Sit by the windows for great people watching along Rainier Avenue or at the bar to chat with the friendly staff.

## 135 THE VELVET ELK

**3605 S McClellan St**
**Mt. Baker** ⑨
**+1 206 717 2902**
*velvet-elk.com*

This bar's name was changed to The Velvet Elk in honor of one of the black velvet paintings on the walls of the establishment. It's a cozy and inviting space, filled with vintage furniture and decor collected by the owner. They serve great cocktails and this is a great, little-known spot to impress a date with. They welcome you to bring in outside food, so you can even grab a pizza from next door Mioposto to enjoy.

## 5 *places for drinks*
# WITH A VIEW

---

**136 SMITH TOWER
OBSERVATORY BAR**
**506 2nd Avenue
Pioneer Square** ②
**+1 206 624 0414**
*smithtower.com/
attractions/
observatory-bar*

No bar in Seattle boasts a view quite like the Smith Tower Observatory Bar's. Unfortunately, those views come at a premium as you need to pay an entry fee (19 dollars) to access the area. We recommend taking their new Talking Tower Tour, which includes all-day access to the Observatory Bar in addition to a guided tour of the historic building, once the tallest building West of the Mississippi!

**137 RAY'S BOATHOUSE**
**6049 Seaview
Avenue NW
Ballard** ⑤
**+1 206 789 3770**
*rays.com*

Ray's is a classic seafood restaurant located just outside of the main part of the Ballard neighborhood, worth the walk or drive over to enjoy their spectacular views of Shilshole Bay, boats leaving from the Ballard Locks and the Olympic Mountains. The upstairs Ray's Cafe is a more casual setting while the Boathouse offers a more upscale dining experience.

## 138 MARINATION MA KAI

**1660 Harbor**
**Avenue SW**
**West Seattle** ⑧
**+1 206 328 8226**
*marinationmobile.com*

Stop by Marination Ma Kai every time you visit Seattle, and see if you can spot the new additions to the city's skyline from their glorious patio. Marination's Hawaiian-Korean food offerings are mouthwatering (get the kimchi fried rice) and their full bar offers plenty to drink alongside. Post up at one of the outdoor picnic tables and watch the West Seattle Water Taxi come and go from the dock next door.

## 139 MBAR

**400 Fairview Avenue**
**N, 14th Floor**
**South Lake Union** ①
**+1 206 457 8287**
*mbarseattle.com*

This chic rooftop bar is worth dressing up for. Not that that's needed in Seattle, but you'll want to look nice for the photographs you'll take with the great views. On the clearest days, you can see the Olympic Mountains, Space Needle, Lake Union all the way to the North Cascades while you enjoy their great 'Levantine hospitality' of elevated food and beverages.

## 140 THE LOOKOUT

**757 Bellevue**
**Avenue E**
**Capitol Hill** ③
**+1 206 922 3767**
*thelookoutbar*
*seattle.com*

The Lookout is a quintessential locals' bar, as it's not particularly conveniently located to other tourist attractions. A walk north from central Capitol Hill to this bar will expand your understanding of the neighborhood, though, and is worth it for the quirky back patio with a view of Lake Union. They've got a great happy hour menu and lots of local beers on tap.

# The 5 best **OUTDOOR**
## *drinking spots*

---

### 141 BALE BREAKER & YONDER CIDER TAPROOM

**826 NW 49th St**
**Ballard** ⑤
**+1 773 998 1464**
*bbycballard.com*

This property has changed hands between a few different purveyors of beer over the years, but the quality of the outdoor space remains the same. Bale Breaker, a Yakima-based brewery, took over recently and has even made some improvements to the massive outdoor seating area. Kids and dogs are everywhere while adults enjoy a wide array of beverages. A great array of different food trucks park nearby almost daily.

### 142 FREMONT BREWERY

**1050 N 34th St**
**Fremont** ⑤
**+1 206 420 2407**
*fremontbrewing.com*

Ten years ago Fremont Brewery was 1/10 its current size, which is hard to believe when you take in their glorious flowering patio and effortless in- and outdoor flow of their current space. Their success is due to a high-quality product (the beers really are great) and killer marketing (you'll want merch from here). Grab a flight to try a few classics (like the Interurban IPA) and enjoy all the people watching outside.

## 143 AMPERSAND CAFE ON ALKI

**2536 Alki Avenue SW**
**Alki** ⑧
**+1 206 466 5254**
*ampersandalki.com*

This small, charming cafe and bakery on Alki Avenue is a great place to get off your feet if you've been busy swimming or walking Alki Beach. They have plenty of tables set up out front across the road from the beach where you can enjoy one of their daily pastry specials and a seasonal drink, like a rosewater cardamom latte.

142 FREMONT BREWERY

## 144 GROWLERZ TAPROOM

5269 Rainier
Avenue S
Hillman City ⑨
+1 206 459 2726
*growlerzseattle.com*

A dog park with beers available for purchase! A more Seattle-like business could not have been created by AI. This space operates as a doggie daycare Monday-Friday. The play area does require a fee (12 dollars per single entry and 100 dollars for an 11-entry pass along with monthly membership options) but it's worth it for the fun of socializing with other dog parents (and enthusiasts) over brews. No dog required to come, just buy a beer.

## 145 OLD STOVE BREWING

1901 Western Avenue
Downtown ②
+1 206 602 6120
*oldstove.com*

Old Stove's Pike Place Market location offers unparalleled views of Puget Sound, the Olympic Mountains and Mount Rainier on a clear day from their ample outdoor seating options. Service is surprisingly efficient even on a busy day, although in the height of tourist season (July-August) it may be hard to get a table. Locals flock here on weekdays for happy hour, especially the first nice days of spring.

# 5 spots with great
# BAR GAMES

---

## 146 SEATTLE TAVERN & POOL HALL

**5811 Airport Way S**
**Georgetown** ⑨
**+1 206 767 1101**
*seattletavern.com*

Come here on a winter evening and you'll feel like you stepped back through time. Neon signs light up the bar and pool tables and there's always plenty of sports on TV if you have to wait your turn for a table. At last check pool rates were pretty affordable compared to other options in town. This is exactly the kind of bar to try Seattle's simplest beer, a Rainier, though they also have plenty of other locals on tap.

## 147 ADD-A-BALL

**315 N 36th St, #2B**
**Fremont** ⑤
*add-a-ball.com*

Add-a-Ball's slogan should be 'a bar game playground for adults.' They boast the largest collection of vintage coin-operated arcade machines in Seattle. A particular highlight for many visitors is Killer Queen, a 10-player arcade game that is surprisingly fun to play even with strangers. Bring some cash for the change machine and play to your heart's content.

## 148 ICE BOX ARCADE

**615 NW Bright St**
**Fremont** ⑤
**+1 206 588 2661**
*iceboxarcade.com*

Ice Box Arcade is tucked away in residential 'Frelard' (the unofficial neighborhood between Fremont and Ballard). You can preview their extensive pinball machines and arcade game offerings online on their website. A bonus if you're traveling with younger folk:, this place is all-ages until 8 pm. They're also the home of Seattle's Belles & Chimes league for women and gender minority pinball players.

## 149 FLATSTICK PUB

**240 2nd Avenue S**
**Pioneer Square** ②
**+1 206 682 0608**
*flatstickpub.com/*
*pioneer-square*

Flatstick Pub has two locations in Seattle, and you can choose your destination based on the weather. If it's a dreary day, head to the Pioneer Square basement location where you won't notice the damp. Head to the SLU location to enjoy larger sculptures from Seattle artist, Ryan Henry Ward. At either spot, you'll enjoy mini golf (and other golf-adjacent games) alongside tons of local beer offerings.

## 150 JUPITER BAR

**2126 2nd Avenue,**
**Suite A**
**Belltown** ①
*jupiterbarseattle.com*

Jupiter Bar is a great spot for a date, with both food and drinks available for purchase while you browse the various games. Their back room is dedicated to pinball and a few other arcade games to help break the ice. They also have art on display by local artists that rotate and a patio out front in case your senses are overstimulated inside by all the activity.

# 5 bars with great
# DRAG SHOWS

---

### 151 ADMIRAL PUB

**2306 California**
**Avenue SW**
**North Admiral** ⑧
**+1 206 933 9500**

Peek in the window of this West Seattle bar and you'll think it's a run-of-the-mill sports bar, but Admiral Pub is so much more than that. There's something going on every night of the week, be it trivia, sports game screening, bingo, karaoke, or the best night of the week, Drag Show Night! No tickets needed for these free shows, just come by and have a good time.

### 152 KREMWERK

**1809 Minor Avenue**
**Downtown** ①
**+1 206 682 2935**
*kremwerk.com*

The Kremwerk, Timber Room and Cherry Complex is a nightclub and live music venue centering queerness and 'progressive electronic music.' They host Seattle's longest running by-and-for transgender and nonbinary produced and casted drag show, designed for trans people to be celebrated and share community with one another.

## 153 JULIA'S ON BROADWAY

300 Broadway E
Capitol Hill ③
+1 206 747 2703
*juliasonbroadway.com*

Julia's hosts the Le Faux drag show, Seattle's longest running drag series. It's a spot where you'll find many bachelor/ette and birthday parties celebrating, along with plenty of first-time drag performance attendees. It is a great place to start if you haven't attended a drag show before: there's a little something in the performances for everyone, including comedy, celebrity impersonators, burlesque and more.

## 154 BOOMBOX BAR

9608 16th
Avenue SW
White Center ⑧
+1 206 557 4671
*boomboxbar.com*

Great drag shows aren't just on Capitol Hill! Head to White Center to Boombox Bar to watch the Boombox Babes strut their stuff regularly. They also host karaoke most nights, viewing parties for sports AND reality TV events, and host a killer Pride party every June. Check their events scheduled for the next show or featured DJ.

## 155 MIMOSAS CABARET

AT: UNICORN
1118 E Pike St
Capitol Hill ③
+1 206 325 6492
*unicornseattle.com/
mimosascabaret*

Everything is better with a mimosa, even a drag show. Check out Unicorn's Mimosas Cabaret most Saturdays and Sundays at this Capitol Hill club. Tickets for the show are 30 dollars and an all you can eat buffet will only set you back another 13 dollars. Unicorn offers tons of other weekly events too, including karaoke, 'gayme' nights and trivia.

# 5 bars to **SING YOUR HEART OUT**

---

## 156 LITTLE RED HEN

**7115 Woodlawn Avenue NE**
**Green Lake** ⑤
**+1 206 522 1168**
*littleredhen.com*

Seattle is not known as a particular haven for country music, but Little Red Hen will try and convince you otherwise. Seattle's best known 'western' bar offers tons of live music and dance lesson nights, in addition to weekly karaoke (usually on Wednesdays). If you're craving country music, look no further than this Green Lake bar, you won't be disappointed.

## 157 ROCK BOX

**1603 Nagle Place**
**Capitol Hill** ③
**+1 206 302 7625**
*rockboxseattle.com*

Located next to Cal Anderson Park on Capitol Hill, Rock Box is a great place to pop into with a group of friends to enjoy a Japanese-style private karaoke room. They have eleven private rooms that can accommodate varying numbers of people. They offer discounts on both room reservation and drinks during happy hours daily and all-day on Sundays.

## 158 SEATTLE'S BEST KARAOKE

**1818 Minor Avenue
Downtown ③
+1 206 343 6599**
*sbkaraoke.com*

Seattle's Best Karaoke offers the chance to rent private karaoke rooms for all ages and there is no age limit for attendance here. This spot in South Lake Union is particularly great for parties, with up to 20 people allowed in select private rooms. You can bring your own food and drinks (including alcohol, with a 10-dollar City of Seattle banquet permit acquired online).

## 159 BURLESKARAOKE
AT: QUEER/BAR

**1518 11th Avenue
Capitol Hill ③**
*thequeerbar.com*

Queer/Bar hosts Burleskaraoke monthly (sometimes more often), a show that combines the skill and entertainment of burlesque artists with the joys of karaoke. There's so much going on you'll hardly know where to look. Check out their event calendar for the next featured artists and be sure to leave your shyness at the door.

## 160 ORIENT EXPRESS

**2963 4th Avenue S
SoDo ⑨
+1 206 682 0683**
*seattleorientexpress.com*

This restaurant and karaoke bar located in SoDo is housed in a series of old train cars salvaged over the years from Seattle City Light. It's a must-visit for Seattle's karaoke fans (and even those who don't love karaoke, because, when is the last time you sang in public *and* ate a meal inside the same refurbished train car?).

# 5 great
# L G B T Q + bars

## 161 WILDROSE

**1021 E Pike St**
**Capitol Hill** ③
**+1 206 324 9210**
*thewildrosebar.com*

There are shockingly few lesbian bars in America (just 27 according to a 2022 count). Wildrose is Seattle's only lesbian bar and it's been in operation since 1984. 'A place for women…and all are welcome' is their motto. They host a wide array of events including drag shows, bingo, trivia and karaoke during which you can enjoy a wide array of drinks.

## 162 THE CUFF COMPLEX

**1533 13th Avenue**
**Capitol Hill** ③
**+1 206 323 1525**
*cuffcomplex.com*

The Cuff Complex is proudly one of the oldest LGBTQ+ clubs in Seattle and calling it a complex does justice to the size of this space. If you're looking for a hot dance floor on a Friday night, head over here. They have four bars and a sizable outdoor patio to post up at when you need to catch your breath and cool down.

## 163 CHANGES BAR & GRILL

**2103 N 45th St**
**Wallingford** ⑤
**+1 206 545 8363**

This small Wallingford neighborhood gay bar is pretty unassuming from the street with the exception of its rainbow logo sign. As you step inside, you might mistake it for just another sports bar, but the staff are friendlier. Even if it's your first time in, you'll be greeted like a local. It's an inviting place to pass a few hours, watching a game and chatting with the staff or playing pool in the back.

## 164 PONY

**1221 E Madison St**
**Capitol Hill** ③
*ponyseattle.com*

Pony is 'a very queer bar' that serves happy hour till 8 pm every night (!). They have a wide array of theme nights and events. First Fridays feature retro gay tunes from 1955-1985, so check the event calendar to find your kind of thing. They have a large patio that's open year-round and west facing so it can be fun to stop in earlier in the evening, too.

## 165 CRESCENT LOUNGE

**1413 E Olive Way**
**Capitol Hill** ③
**+1 206 659 4476**

Crescent Lounge is a divey gay bar right on the edge of Capitol Hill, featuring tons of opportunities for karaoke and a wide range of clientele. They're proud to call themselves the oldest gay and dive bar in the city, open since 1948. Order your drink of choice and enjoy listening to the many regulars belt their hearts out.

FILSON

# 80 PLACES TO SHOP

---

5 locally loved **BOOKSTORES** —————————— 106

5 **OUTDOOR GEAR** and **CLOTHING** stores —— 108

5 great **FARMERS MARKETS** —————————— 110

5 groovy **RECORD STORES** —————————— 113

5 great **HOBBY STORES** —————————— 115

The 5 best **WEED SHOPS** —————————— 117

5 fun places for random **GIFT SHOPPING** ——— 119

5 of the best **BOTTLE SHOPS** —————————— 122

5 things **MADE IN
AND AROUND SEATTLE** —————————— 124

5 places for **PLANT** people —————————— 127

5 locally loved **FURNITURE STORES** ————— 130

5 CLOTHING *shops to pinpoint*
SEATTLE STYLE —————————————— 132

5 *great* THRIFT *and* VINTAGE
CLOTHING *shops* —————————————— 134

5 *spots for your next* TATTOO —————————— 136

5 *great independent* JEWELRY STORES ————— 138

5 *places to* PAMPER YOURSELF ——————— 140

# 5 locally loved
# BOOKSTORES

## 166 ADA'S TECHNICAL BOOKS AND CAFÉ

425 15th Avenue E
Capitol Hill ③
+1 206 322 1058
adasbooks.com

Ada's tagline is 'for the cravings of the technical mind.' Even if you don't consider yours a 'technical mind' you'll find something to interest you in Ada's wide array of science (and adjacent) books and media. The attached vegetarian cafe is a great place to post up with your latest purchase and they offer lots of interesting events on a regular basis, most regularly a kid's reading hour on weekends.

## 167 ELLIOTT BAY BOOK COMPANY

1521 10th Avenue
Capitol Hill ③
+1 206 624 6600
elliottbaybook.com

Elliott Bay Book Company is an oasis of knowledge and comfort in the bustling heart of Capitol Hill. They have an excellent PNW section, with books to help you better appreciate the history, natural wonders and authors of Seattle and the surrounding area. The helpdesk staff are particularly friendly and will help you find your next favorite read or the perfect gift.

## 168 THIRD PLACE BOOKS

5041 Wilson
Avenue S
Seward Park ⑨
+1 206 474 2200
thirdplacebooks.com

Third Place Books has three locations dotted around Seattle: their Lake Forest Park location boasts up to 200.000 new, used, and bargain books for sale. The newest location (opened in 2016) in Seward Park, recently added on a Chuck's Hop Shop outpost where you can enjoy a beverage while you peruse your latest literary purchase. All three locations have a robust used book buying program, though you need to make an appointment in order to sell.

## 169 PAPER BOAT BOOKSELLERS

6040 California
Avenue SW, Suite A
West Seattle ⑧
+1 206 743 8283
paperboatbook
sellers.com

This quaint bookstore in West Seattle packs a great vibe into a small storefront. The young adult and kid's section take up a decent portion of the store, offering plenty for young browsers. They host events with local authors, a weekly family readers series, and meetings of a few book clubs as well. If you can't find what you're looking for, the friendly staff will place orders for you.

## 170 OPEN BOOKS A POEM EMPORIUM

108 Cherry St
Pioneer Square ②
+1 206 633 0811
openpoetrybooks.com

This small, quaint bookstore in Pioneer Square is a welcome recent addition to Seattle's literary scene. They offer a selection of rare, out-of-print poetry books, chapbooks, and journals. They offer a great recommendation service via email or when you're shopping in-store. For those trying to get some remote work done while you're in town, you can book their Parlor Room for coworking hours.

# 5 OUTDOOR GEAR and CLOTHING stores

## 171 ASCENT OUTDOORS

5209 Ballard
Avenue NW
Ballard ⑤
+1 206 545 8810
ascentoutdoors.com

This smaller (but still full-service) outdoor retail store is a great place to go in Ballard when you want to get advice from experts on biking, skiing, climbing, hiking or mountaineering. Their store also includes a secondhand section and in 2019 they began offering guided outdoor adventures as well.

172 REI FLAGSHIP STORE

## 172 REI FLAGSHIP STORE

222 Yale Avenue N
South Lake Union ①
+1 206 223 1944
rei.com/stores/seattle

Recreational Equipment, Inc. (REI) was founded in 1938 by a group of climbing friends and is still a member-owned co-op today. The Flagship store in Seattle is well worth a visit for a bike tune up, gear rental or purchase, or for an event or climbing session on their 65-feet-tall Pinnacle climbing wall.

## 173 WONDERLAND GEAR EXCHANGE

122 NW 36th St
Fremont ⑤
+1 206 582 1987
wonderlandgearex-
change.com

First time adventurers and experienced outdoorists alike will appreciate the chance to buy and sell used gear here. They focus on consigning seasonally relevant gear that's 5-7 years old or less and their new(ish) location in Fremont has allowed them to expand their inventory.

## 174 OUTDOOR RESEARCH

2203 1st Avenue S
SoDo ⑨
+1 206 268 7325
outdoorresearch.com

Outdoor research became an adventurer's household name in the 80s and 90s for their focus on quality and functional USA-manufactured outdoor gear. Their Flagship store in the SoDo neighborhood is well worth a visit, as can be their outlet store just south of Seattle in Des Moines.

## 175 FEATHERED FRIENDS

263 Yale Avenue N
South Lake Union ①
+1 206 292 2210
featheredfriends.com

Feathered friends has been handcrafting high-quality down products for outdoor activities (and now beyond) in Seattle since 1972. 100% of the down they use is certified for the Responsible Down Standard (RDS). Their geoduck camping pillow is a great low-cost entry point to begin to understand the coziness of their products.

## 5 great
# FARMERS MARKETS

---

### 176 FREMONT SUNDAY STREET MARKET

3401 Evanston
Avenue N
Fremont ⑤
fremontmarket.com

The Fremont Sunday market is a bustling weekly event with more than 100 rotating and regular vendors selling meals, locally made crafts, vintage goods and antiques. It's the perfect place to pick up a souvenir from your travels, or shop for artwork or the finishing piece of furniture for your new Seattle pad. It's a family-owned organization that strives to support local businesses in the heart of Fremont.

### 177 WEST SEATTLE FARMERS MARKET

SW Alaska St
& California
Avenue SW
The Junction ⑧
+1 206 632 5234
seattlefarmers
markets.org/wsfm

A section of California Avenue shuts down every Sunday (year-round) for the West Seattle Farmers market, which is smaller than the behemoth of Ballard but draws a lot more locals than tourists. There are several food vendors (and tons of nearby restaurants) plus of course lots of local fish, meat and produce to inspire your next home-cooked meal.

176 FREMONT SUNDAY STREET MARKET

177 WEST SEATTLE FARMERS MARKET

## 178 BALLARD FARMERS MARKET

5345 Ballard
Avenue NW
Ballard ⑤
sfmamarkets.com/
visit-ballard-farmers-
market

The Sunday Ballard Farmers Market has expanded each year, now stretching from Ballard Avenue onto 22nd Avenue towards NW Market Street. In addition to a plethora of local produce (all grown only in Washington State), there are lots of craft vendors, canned goods and artwork for sale. Streetside businesses open their doors wide and often push merchandise onto the sidewalks, almost overwhelming your purchase-decision-making process!

## 179 CAPITOL HILL FARMERS MARKET

E Barbara Bailey Way
Capitol Hill ③
+1 206 547 2278
seattlefarmers
markets.org/chfm

The Capitol Hill Farmers Market operates year-round on Sundays from 11 am to 3 pm and on Tuesdays in the summer from mid-July through September from 3 to 7 pm. It's located on E Denny Way, between Broadway and 10th Avenue E. It offers a wide array of produce, other locally grown and produced foods, as well as some craft and decor items for purchase.

## 180 COLUMBIA CITY FARMERS MARKET

37th Avenue S
Columbia City ⑨
+1 206 632 5234
seattlefarmers
markets.org/ccfm

The Columbia City Farmers Market is a great place to shop on Wednesday nights between May and mid-October. A short walk from the Columbia City light rail station, you can find fresh produce and meals. Grab ingredients for picnicking in nearby Columbia Park or walk a mile to the shores of Lake Washington to enjoy your purchases. In the winters the market operates every other Saturday.

# 5 *groovy*
# RECORD STORES

## 181 EASY STREET RECORDS

4559 California
Avenue SW
The Junction ⑧
+1 206 938 3279
easystreetonline.com

Easy Street Records has it all, a great record collection to shop from, awesome events with locally and nationally famous artists, a small stage for performances in the evening and a booming cafe that serves awesome breakfast and lunch daily from 7 am to 3 pm.

181 EASY STREET RECORDS

## 182 SILVER PLATTERS SODO

2930 1st Avenue S
SoDo ⑨
+1 206 283 3472
silverplatters.com

Silver Platters is the place to go if you're a fan of music and video outside the digital realm. They have an enormous vinyl collection in addition to CDs and DVDs, and claim their selection is the largest in the Northwest. There's a buy-back program where you can sell your used items as well. They have two other locations in Bellevue and Lynwood, but SoDo offers the most variety.

## 183 DAYBREAK RECORDS

4323 Fremont
Avenue N
Fremont ⑤
+1 206 268 0702
daybreakrecord
store.com

Daybreak Records caters to the modern record-buying community with a carefully curated selection of new and used vinyl. Their converted storefront in Fremont has a listening station so you can try before you buy. They purchase used albums and 45s in exchange for store credit.

## 184 SONIC BOOM RECORDS

2209 NW Market St
Ballard ⑤
+1 206 297 2666
sonicboomrecords.com

Be sure to pop into Sonic Boom Records while you're enjoying the other great shops along Market Street NW and nearby Ballard Avenue. Their enterprise took off after they hosted local darlings Death Cab for Cutie for an in-store performance after the release of their 1998 debut album.

## 185 FAT CAT RECORDS

4515 Meridian
Avenue N
Wallingford ⑤
+1 206 547 5799
fatcatrecordsus.com

Located in the Wallingford neighborhood, this family-run record store sells new and used records, CDs and tapes catering to a wide array of music tastes. They do a lot of used record buying (in addition to stereo equipment) and will even offer house calls.

# 5 *great*
# HOBBY STORES

---

## 186 NORTHWEST ART & FRAME

4733 California
Avenue SW
The Junction ⑧
+1 206 937 5507
nwartandframe.com

Whether you're shopping for a card and small gift for a friend or family member, looking to have a piece of art of photography framed, or a burgeoning artist looking to restock your supplies – you'll find it all at Northwest Art & Frame in West Seattle. They stock a wide variety of inspiration for your next creative project along with all the tools to make it happen.

## 187 PHOTOGRAPHIC CENTER NORTHWEST

900 12th Avenue
Capitol Hill ③
+1 206 720 7222
pcnw.org

Photographic Center Northwest wants 'photographic education for everyone.' They offer classes for all levels of photographers on both technical instruction and creative/artistic development. From a full certificate program, 10-week courses, to single-day workshops, there's something for photographers of all skill levels and schedule flexibility. Their gallery has an exhibit open to the public that rotates quarterly.

## 188 STITCHES
711 E Pike St
Capitol Hill ③
+1 206 709 0707
stitchesseattle.com

Stitches on Capitol Hill offers fabric, yarn, kits and buttons for sale, focusing on interesting and new products and pitches itself as *not your normal fabric store*. Their staff are friendly and helpful when brainstorming the right fit for your next project. They used to offer several classes prior to the pandemic; hopefully they'll start up again soon.

## 189 THE WORKS
512 2nd Avenue
Pioneer Square ②
+1 206 475 5974
theworksseattle.com

The Works in Pioneer Square believes 'everyone is wildly creative'. Even if you don't feel wildly creative, you should check out their schedule because there's sure to be something you're intrigued to learn. From macraweave, to bookbinding, to embroidering wildflower hats, there's a new skill waiting to be learned at The Works Seattle.

## 190 SEVEN HILLS RUNNING SHOP
3139 W Government
Way, Suite B
Magnolia ④
+1 206 683 2532
sevenhillsrunning
shop.com

This running store is a bit off the beaten path, nestled in the Magnolia neighborhood, but it's the first stop you should make if you're interested in trying trail running for the first time. Their store group-runs leave the shop at 6.30 pm every Tuesday to enjoy nearby Discovery Park. It's also a great spot if you need a new pair of running or walking sneakers during your travels.

# *The 5 best* **WEED SHOPS**

## 191 **RUCKUS RECREATIONAL**

1463 E Republican St
Capitol Hill ③
+1 206 257 4805
*ruckusrec.com*

Located on the slightly less chaotic side of Capitol Hill, Ruckus Recreational is a favorite weed shop of locals. The staff are notoriously friendly and helpful, and they stock plenty from local growers at all price ranges. They have a fun backstory about the store name on their website and this location directly competes with another, less-locally-loved weed store just across the street.

## 192 **DOCKSIDE CANNIBAS**

4601 Leary Way NW
Ballard ⑤
+1 206 350 2053
*docksidecannabis.com*

Dockside Cannabis now boasts four locations, three in Seattle and one in Shoreline. The Ballard location is an attractive, light-filled storefront, albeit in a pretty industrial part of Ballard. They're a woman and minority-owned company that is working to serve both medical and recreational clients at all their locations while 'righting the wrongs of 100 years of prohibition.'

## 193 KUSHKLUB

20019 Aurora
Avenue N, Suite B
Shoreline
+1 206 403 1757
kushklub.com

KushKlub is a well-regarded cannabis dispensary in Shoreline, just north of Seattle. They have different 'daily deals' every day of the week to meet the needs of all kinds of recreational users. On Thursday, you can even choose any of the deals from any other day of the week! They also participate 'in programs to ensure responsible cannabis integration and programs focused on restorative justice.'

## 194 OZ. CANNABIS

3831 Stone Way N
Fremont ⑤
+1 206 251 0630
ozseattle.com

OZ. is Fremont's oldest licensed cannabis dispensary, open since 2015. They pride themselves on super clear product information and helpful staff, working to make sure every customer leaves with what they were looking for at the best price. They encourage customers to support several nonprofits (all listed on their website) that are working towards restorative justice and ending the war on drugs.

## 195 KEMP'S WEED SHOP

3035 1st Avenue
Belltown ①
+1 206 345 0009
kempscannabis.com

Shawn Kemp is a local celebrity in Seattle and a former professional basketball player for Seattle's long-since-departed SuperSonics. Unfortunately, recent brushes with the law taint a bit of his celebrity, though his weed shop is still one of the best in the city. With two locations now, the Belltown one is more convenient to the rest of the city and has a great selection with some good deals.

# 5 fun places for random
# GIFT SHOPPING

## 196 ARCHIE MCPHEE

1300 N 45th St
Wallingford ⑤
+1 206 297 0240
*archiemcphee*
*seattle.com*

Archie McPhee is the kind of store you pop into when you're looking for a silly gift for a friend or family member and walk out with four gifts for four different people, along with something random and kind of weird for yourself. While you can browse and purchase from their wide selection online, the Seattle Store is worth a visit for the fun and randomness you'll encounter.

## 197 STANDARD GOODS

501 E Pike St
Capitol Hill ③
+1 206 323 0207
*thestandardgoods.com*

Standard Goods is a lifestyle boutique that has two locations in Seattle, one in Ballard and one on Capitol Hill, as well as a third location in Naperville, Illinois. They sell products from a large array of local vendors and definitely work hard to maintain their PNW hipster vibe. Pick up a piece of clothing, art or sticker (so many stickers!) to remember your travels by.

198 PRISM

## 198 PRISM

5208 Ballard
Avenue NW
Ballard ⑤
+1 206 402 4706
prismseattle.com

Prism is one of the more stylish and varied independent boutiques on Ballard Avenue NW in the main shopping area of the Ballard neighborhood. They offer both men's and women's clothing, in addition to accessories and eclectic decor, home goods and reading materials. It's a great stop on your way to or from the Ballard Farmers Market.

## 199 STUHLBERGS

1801 Queen Anne
Avenue N
Queen Anne ④
+1 206 352 2351
stuhlbergs.com

Stuhlbergs is a gift shop and children's boutique in a turn-of-the-century home at the top of Queen Anne hill. The owner, Megan Stuhlberg Mahapatra, reportedly carefully curates the whole collection. You'll likely walk out with something different than you walked in for (or perhaps three times more than you intended to purchase) but that's half the fun.

## 200 MEEPLES GAMES

3727 California
Avenue SW, Suite 2B
North Admiral ⑧
+1 206 535 7896
meeplesgames.com

Meeples Games is 'your friendly neighborhood gaming store' located in West Seattle. Their selection isn't gigantic, but you'll likely find what you want and the staff are fun and helpful. They have a gaming cafe where you'll always find a group or two playing some kind of role-playing game. Their online events calendar showcases a ton of chances to get involved, including weekly open D&D sessions.

# 5 of the best
# BOTTLE SHOPS

## 201 THE BEER JUNCTION

4511 California
Avenue SW
The Junction ⑧
+1 206 938 2337
*thebeerjunction.com*

The Beer Junction in West Seattle is
a great destination for beer lovers.
They have a wide variety of refrigerated
beers for purchase in the back half
of the premises. Keep an eye on their
Instagram for their latest arrivals.
They also host 35+ taps where you can
try things before you buy them. Their
seasonal beer events are absolutely
worth marking in your calendar.

## 202 A1 HOP SHOP

10406 Greenwood
Avenue N
Greenwood ⑦
+1 206 789 7293
*a1hopshop.com*

A dear friend of this author is an expert
on barrel-aged bears and reports that A1
Hop Shop on 104th has *the* best selection
of these kinds of brews in all of Seattle, so
if you're into the darker, funkier side of
beer, definitely add this place to your list.
The business is woman-owned and also
offers a wide array of other beers, wines
and seltzers. They do keep 15-20 beers on
tap so you can stick around and try
a brew on their patio.

## 203 FULL THROTTLE BOTTLES

5909 Airport Way S
Georgetown ⑨
+1 206 763 2079

Full Throttle Bottles offers a good selection of beers and wines in Seattle's Georgetown neighborhood. Like most bottle shops these days, they also offer a pub-y area to sit down and taste things straight from their taps. If you're not sure what you're looking for, the staff here will definitely help you find your next favorite beverage.

## 204 PIKE & WESTERN

1934 Pike Place
Downtown ②
+1 206 441 1307
pikeandwestern.com

The Pike & Western wine shop is located adjacent to Pike Place Market in downtown Seattle, so it's an easy stop after you check out other tourist attractions. They curate a wine collection that always manages to have a few truly affordable options and several worth-saving-for-a-celebration bottles. Talk to whoever is working that day to get a good recommendation.

## 205 PORTALIS WINE SHOP

6754 15th
Avenue NW
Ballard ⑤
+1 206 783 2007
portaliswines.com

Portalis is located just north of the main drag of the Ballard neighborhood. They focus on offering small-batch wines from all over the world, with several hundred options available in the shop on a given day. The owners clearly enjoy educating their customers, whether they're new to wine or longtime fans, about the makers and intricacies of the wines they sell.

# 5 things MADE IN AND AROUND SEATTLE

## 206 FUNKO POPS

2802 Wetmore
Avenue
Everett
+1 425 783 3616
funko.com

Whether you know it or not, you've likely seen a Funko Pop in the last five years. They took the world by storm as these small, goofy toys started taking up shelves of purchasers of all ages. Their factory and global headquarters are just north of Seattle in Everett, Washington. You can visit the retail store there for a huge variety of Funkos to take home to your Funko-loving kids (or adult friends).

## 207 FILSON

1741 1st Avenue S
SoDo ⑨
+1 206 622 3147
filson.com/store-
locator/seattle-store.html

Filson began creating apparel and gear for outdoor enthusiasts and workers in 1897. Their original customers were those participating in the Yukon Gold Rush and passing through Seattle on their way to Alaska. Stop into their Seattle Flagship store in SoDo to admire their wide array of goods, or if you're pressed for time, pick up a souvenir on your way out of town at the SeaTac airport store.

## 208 BOEING FACTORY: FUTURE OF FLIGHT

8415 Paine Field
Boulevard
Mukilteo
+1 800 464 1476
boeingfuture
offlight.com

"If it ain't Boeing, I ain't going" was a common phrase of this jet manufacturer's loyalists. Boeing has long since moved its headquarters from Seattle, but the company's impact on the city can still be felt today. Head to their Future of Flight exhibit in Mukilteo at Paine Field, approximately 25 miles north of the city, to learn more and appreciate how far flight has come in 100 years.

## 209 FAST PENNY SPIRITS

1138 W Ewing St,
Suite B
Queen Anne ④
+1 206 627 0272
fastpennyspirits.com

You probably don't think *amaro* when you think of Seattle, but those interested in a non-beer alcohol experience in Seattle should definitely head to Fast Penny Spirits. Their distillery and tasting room is located near the Ballard bridge, on the Queen Anne side. For just 35 dollars you can enjoy their VIP experience, including a tour of the facilities, sampling of their latest offerings and a cocktail on their deck.

## 210 PIKE ST. PRESS

1510 Alaskan Way
Downtown ②
+1 206 971 0120
pikestreetpress.com

Conveniently located in Pike Place Market, you can stop in Pike St. Press any time during your visit to Seattle to pick up a locally designed and printed piece of art or greeting card. With plenty of locally themed postcards, you'll have no excuse for not keeping up on your correspondence or letting friends and family know how your trip is going.

# 5 places for
# **PLANT** *people*

---

### 211 **SWANSONS NURSERY**

9701 15th
Avenue NW
Crown Hill ⑦
+1 206 782 2543
swansonsnursery.com

Swansons Nursery is the garden center
Seattleites visit for all their outdoor and
indoor plant needs. It's tucked away in
north Crown Hill, meaning you'll have
to make an effort to get there. But it's
worth the trek to explore the wide array
of native, ornamental and edible plants.
Make an excursion out of your visit and
get a coffee or pastry at the cafe.

### 212 **BOOSH**

2311 S Jackson St
Central District ③
+1 206 491 8560
boosh-plant-nursery.
business.site

This small, chic indoor plant store
in the Central District is a great place
to pop into to find your next favorite
houseplant. The industrial storefront is
transformed inside by trailing pothos
and philodendrons, blooming peace lilies
and growing ficus and dracaenas. They
have a decent selection of containers as
well, making it a good spot to stop for
a housewarming present.

214 SEATTLE PLANT DADDY

## 213 BLUE POPPY FLORAL

8507 35th Avenue NE
Wedgwood ⑥
+1 206 992 0739
bluepoppyfloral.com

This immigrant and woman-owned business in the Wedgwood neighborhood has a lovely storefront with tropical house plants and floral arrangements. They offer a subscription-style service for those interested in regularly available fresh arrangements for the home and delivery is available for a modest fee. They also specialize in arrangements for weddings and other special events.

## 214 SEATTLE PLANT DADDY

1325 N 46th St, Suite B
Wallingford ⑤
+1 206 586 3131
seattleplantdaddy.com

This is the indoor plant store that many millennial dreams are made of. Seattle Plant Daddy's Wallingford store location offers a wide variety of houseplants, including rare and exotic types as well as cacti and succulents. It might be best to arrive with a plan for what plants you're seeking here, otherwise you'll probably walk out with several more than you intended.

## 215 WEST SEATTLE NURSERY & GARDEN CENTER

5275 California Avenue SW
West Seattle ⑧
+1 206 935 9276
westseattlenursery.com

West Seattle's garden store is a fun visit even if you aren't working on a particular plant project at the moment. It's just a block from a great vegan restaurant and a wine tasting room, so you can nourish yourself before or after you peruse the wide array of indoor and outdoor plants. Late spring is a particularly fun time to visit, when the rhododendrons for sale are in bloom.

## *5 locally loved*
# FURNITURE STORES

---

### 216 DIGS

2002 NW Market St
Ballard ⑤
+1 206 457 5709
digsshowroom.com

There is quite a bit of good shopping in Ballard, so while you're there be sure to head east on NW Market Street to stroll through Digs, a local family-owned furniture and decor store. There's tons of PNW-themed gifts for souvenir purchasing, but also some beautiful outdoor and indoor furniture if you've just moved into a new place.

### 217 BALLARD CONSIGNMENT STORE

5459 Leary
Avenue NW
Ballard ⑤
+1 206 859 9956
ballardconsignment.com

Even if you aren't looking for furniture, a wander through Ballard Consignment Store is always a fun afternoon activity, in between other shopping and dining adventures in Ballard. You'll find decor of all styles, from your grandmother's ancient (but beautiful) dining sets to overstock items from well-known modern furniture brands.

## 218 KASALA OUTLET

1946 Occidental
Avenue S
SoDo ⑨
+1 206 340 4112
kasala.com

Kasala is *the* Seattle furniture store, showing up in homes all over the region for more than three decades. While many of the beautiful pieces in their flagship store near Pike Place Market might be out of the average person's price range, the outlet stores in SoDo and Southcenter are the place to start your shopping.

## 219 TIRTO FURNITURE

1908 E Mercer St
Capitol Hill ③
+1 206 322 0597
tirtofurniture.com

This family-owned business on Capitol Hill was inspired by one of the owner's father's collection of Indonesian antiques when he was growing up. They now produce all their handcrafted, teak and rosewood furniture in Blitar, Java, Indonesia and proudly share on their website the benefits they provide their staff. You can browse their offerings online but it's worth a visit in store to appreciate the beauty of these pieces.

## 220 COUCH

5304 Ballard
Avenue NW
Ballard ⑤
+1 206 633 6108
couchseattle.com

Their USA-made couches can be designed down to the tiniest detail. The showroom in Ballard is worth browsing even if you aren't in the market for furniture, as the folks are friendly and you'll be astounded by the variety there can be in couches. You might have to wait a bit for your delivery, though you can also check their clearance offerings for items available right now.

# 5 **CLOTHING** *shops to pinpoint* **SEATTLE STYLE**

---

## 221 **MYSTERY MADE CO.**

4312 SW Oregon St
The Junction ⑧
+1 206 669 9629
mysterymade.com

This 'gentlemen's boutique' is located in the junction area of West Seattle. If you're looking for a gift for a man in your life, this is a great place to start with plenty of clothing and accessory options, in addition to some art and other local goods. The staff is friendly and the prices are reasonable for boutiques in this modern age.

## 222 **SEPTEMBER SHOP**

5410 22nd
Avenue NW
Ballard ⑤
+1 206 420 8119
septembertheshop.com

This Ballard store is a classic PNW hipster boutique, with eye-catching displays in every corner. They offer both men's and women's fashions, in addition to accessories and a selection of trendy home goods. The colors on display are always decidedly suited for the Northwest, so if you show up in Seattle without an outfit you're happy with (or your suitcase gets lost en route) head here for an outfit update.

## 223 JACKSTRAW INC

1930 1st Avenue
Belltown ②
+1 206 462 6236
jstraw.com

This upscale, minimalist boutique sits on the south end of the Belltown neighborhood. They offer both men's and women's clothing and are particularly interested in getting to know what their clients want from their wardrobes to help set them on the right path. They offer consulting appointments, but of course an easy way to get inspired is just to stroll through their appealing store.

## 224 FREEMAN

713 Broadway E
Capitol Hill ③
+1 206 327 9932
freemanseattle.com

Freeman is the rare local clothing shop that actually sews its goods in Seattle! They offer a wide variety of menswear along with accessories and self-care products, but they're best known for their first ever product, the Freeman Raincoat. The owners started the company in their kitchen in 2011, pop into their Capitol Hill storefront to appreciate how far they have come since then.

## 225 GLASSWING SHOP

1525 Melrose Avenue
Capitol Hill ③
+1 206 641 7646
glasswingshop.com

Stepping into this shop will make you want to redecorate your home and closet. It's meticulously arranged and filled with plants in a way that makes you feel like you're in your most stylish friend's apartment, rather than a store. Whether you're looking for a plant, a piece of trendy jewelry or a wardrobe refresh, you can find it at Glasswing.

# 5 great
# THRIFT and VINTAGE CLOTHING shops

---

### 226 LUCKY DOG CLOTHING

8201 Greenwood
Avenue N
Greenwood ⑤
+1 206 784 6374
*luckydog.clothing*

Lucky Dog is a menswear thrift store with two locations, one in Greenwood and one in the University District. Their mascot (and logo) is an adorable English bulldog named Squish, who you could run across at either location. Call ahead to either shop to set up an appointment to sell your clothes; they focus on mid to high-end brands.

### 227 THE BARN OWL VINTAGE GOODS

6012 12th Avenue S
Georgetown ⑨
+1 206 486 5442
*barnowlseattle.com*

Hailed by local media as one of Seattle's best vintage stores, The Barn Owl is a great place to stop in the next time you're in the Georgetown neighborhood. The staff are friendly and can help you find what you might be looking for. They offer both men's and women's vintage clothing, with a whole section for vintage Filson goods.

## 228 PRETTY PARLOR

119 Summit
Avenue E
Capitol Hill ③
+1 206 405 2883
prettyparlor.com

Since this Capitol Hill store opened in 2001 they've been focused on selling both new and vintage clothing and accessories originating from the 1920s through the 1990s. It's a distinctly pink and frilly storefront, so be sure to stop in when you're in that kind of mood, before or after a glass of rose nearby.

## 229 FREMONT VINTAGE MALL

3419 Fremont
Avenue N
Fremont ⑤
+1 206 329 4460
fremontvintagemall.com

"The coolest vintage store in the center of the universe" is a pretty bold claim, but this basement vintage store in Fremont certainly delivers on variety. Their collection of sellers offer mid-century furniture, clothing, art, records and decor or *bric-a-brac* as they call it. You really need to just stop in to appreciate it all.

## 230 BON VOYAGE VINTAGE

110 S Washington St
Pioneer Square ②
+1 206 226 5069
bonvoyagevintage.
myshopify.com

Bon Voyage Vintage is bursting at the seams with secondhand and vintage clothing and accessories. Their Pioneer Square shop focuses on clothes from the 1950s-1990s as well as a small selection of newer, locally designed clothing, art and accessories. The owners are fun and vibrant people, always happy to help you find what you might be looking for.

# 5 spots for your next
# TATTOO

## 231 TRUE LOVE TATTOO & ART GALLERY

421 E Pine St
Capitol Hill ③
+1 206 227 3572
trueloveart.com

This proudly gay-owned tattoo parlor on Capitol Hill offers an opportunity to get your tattoo 'without judgment or an intimidating attitude.' They also offer inspiration for your next ink in the form of the rotating local art exhibits featured on their wall that change on a regular basis. Appointments here are required and their artist portfolios can be viewed online.

## 232 DARK HORSE TATTOO

159 Denny Way,
Suite 104
Belltown ①
+1 206 972 8287
darkhorsetattooing.com

Dark Horse Tattoo is an extremely well-regarded collective of tattoo artists located just between the Belltown and Seattle Center neighborhoods. They have been known to accommodate walk-ins, but it's still a best practice to call ahead and schedule a consultation for your custom design. Their website shows off a number of intricate sleeve tattoos that just might inspire your next ink.

### 233 LAUGHING BUDDHA SEATTLE

1121 E Union St
Capitol Hill ③
+1 206 329 8274
laughingbuddha
tattoo.com

If you pop into Laughing Buddha to peruse their jewelry for sale, you just might also walk out with a great idea for a tattoo. They invite shop visitors to chat with their 'body art consultants' about ideas or questions you have for your next tattoo. Their tattoo artists do book quite a ways out, so submit a consultation online if you're in a hurry.

### 234 STORM BLOOM TATTOO

3100 Airport Way S,
Unit 204
SoDo ⑨
stormbloomtattoo.com

Storm Bloom Tattoo is located in the old Rainier Brewery in SoDo. In addition to tattoo artistry, they also offer design services (maybe your original idea for a tattoo is now something you'd prefer as a piece of art?). Their current artist has a wide portfolio that focuses on 'traditional work with a folksy twist' available for browsing on their website.

### 235 SIDE QUEST TATTOO

617 E Pike St
Capitol Hill ③
+1 206 323 4657
sidequesttattoo.com

With eleven or more tattoo artists in residence, you're sure to find someone here whose style resonates with what you're looking for in a tattoo. They do occasionally allow walk-ins, though it's not advertised on their website. As always with a tattoo though, spend some time perusing the great variety of styles of their artists to find the best fit.

## *5 great independent*
# JEWELRY STORES

---

**236 VALERIE MADISON**

1422 34th Avenue
Madrona ③
+1 206 395 6359
*valeriemadison.com*

This author may have had to unsubscribe from emails from Valerie Madison, because their offerings are just too tempting to receive on a weekly basis. Valerie Madison's contemporary and classically inspired jewelry is particularly special for weddings and engagements, but she also offers a line of earrings and necklaces for more everyday occasions.

**237 GREEN LAKE JEWELRY WORKS**

550 NE Northgate Way
Northgate ⑦
+1 206 527 1108
*greenlakejewelry.com*

While neither of their two locations are actually in Green Lake anymore, the company's original location was when it opened in 1996. Now, the stores in both Northgate and Bellevue are truly almost overwhelming to walk into. Jewelry fans will have a hard time walking out empty-handed. The company is best known for its custom jewelry designs, and many a happy local engagement began here.

## 238 BALEEN

6418 20th Avenue NW
Ballard ⑤
shopbaleen.com

Baleen offers handmade jewelry made in a zero-waste facility in Seattle. While you may see their jewelry at a variety of different stores and markets, their North Ballard storefront is a great place to check out all their offerings in one place. While there are plenty of affordable jewelry companies in the market, why not buy locally while you're here in Seattle?

## 239 BARAKA GEMS

8218 Greenwood
Avenue N
Greenwood ⑤
+1 206 783 1313
barakagems.com

Baraka Gems has origins in the community dating back 40+ years and they pride themselves on being a welcoming store, dedicated to creating special moments for all customers and honoring those who decide to sell jewelry or gems to them as well. With a lovely selection of vintage items, as well as the chance to design your own pieces, the sky's the limit at this lovely Greenwood store.

## 240 AIDE-MÉMOIRE

7003 3rd Avenue NW
Phinney Ridge ⑤
+1 314 441 5173
a-m.shop

Aide-mémoire was opened by its owner, Aran Galligan, who wanted to make handcrafted jewelry in an ethical and environmentally friendly way. While they don't offer fully custom orders, their modified and bespoke options mean you can make many pieces feel truly unique to you. Their Phinney Ridge storefront also offers a selection of handcrafted, environmentally or socially conscious gifts by local Seattle makers.

## 5 places to
# PAMPER YOURSELF

**241 SACRED RAIN HEALING CENTER**

1100 NW 50th St
Ballard ⑤
+1 206 789 6288
sacredrainhealing.com

Sacred Rain works to take you away from the busy surrounding city and leave your troubles at the door. They pride themselves as being Seattle's only all-gender, clothing-optional health spa. They have both indoor and outdoor lounge spaces, a cedar sauna, outdoor hot pool, cold showers, a variety of massage and bodywork services, and special events and activities.

**242 ANANYA SPA SEATTLE**

2810 Elliott Avenue
Belltown ①
+1 206 217 1744
ananyaspaseattle.com

Ananya is a woman-owned day spa in Belltown (just north of Downtown Seattle) that offers many classic day spa treatments including massages, facials, skin treatments and waxing services. They have a number of packages for the ultimate day of indulging and seasonal specials. They're regularly ranked as one of the top spas in Seattle for good reason and the staff are very friendly.

## 243 HABITUDE

2801 NW Market St
Ballard ⑤
+1 206 782 2898
habitude.com

This Aveda spa, salon and gallery in Ballard can pamper you in pretty much any way you need. Their upstairs spa facilities are cozy and calming while the bright and airy salon downstairs is always buzzing with activities and the hum of hair dryers. They offer a variety of packages for all-day pampering if you're feeling particularly indulgent.

## 244 THE LADIES ROOM

8538 1st Avenue NW
Greenwood ⑤
+1 206 466 2374
ladiesroom206.com

The Ladies Room in Greenwood offers women multiple soaking pools, saunas, and a eucalyptus steam room as well as a-la-carte add-ons (appointments required) for massages, facials and body scrubs. Walk-ins welcome Tue-Thu but appointments are required for all visits on Friday, Saturdays and Sundays. All genders are welcome on Wednesdays.

## 245 HOTHOUSE SPA & SAUNA

1019 E Pike St
Capitol Hill ③
+1 206 568 3240
hothousespa.com

Hothouse Spa & Sauna is a private rental spa in the heart of Seattle on Capitol Hill, open seven days a week for private use by all genders. You can make a reservation for up to eight people to enjoy the hot tub, cedar sauna, herbal steam room, cold plunge shower and relaxation area with friends or family. Additional fees apply for reservations for more than four guests.

THE SPHERES

# 25 BUILDINGS TO ADMIRE

5 HISTORIC *buildings* —————————— 144

5 BRIDGES *to walk (or ride) across* ————— 146

5 iconic SEATTLE LANDMARKS ————— 149

5 *interesting architecture and building* TOURS —— 152

5 QUIRKY *buildings & structures* ————— 154

# 5 HISTORIC *buildings*

### 246 DENNY HALL

Klickitat Lane
UDistrict ⑥
*washington.edu*

Denny Hall was the first building constructed on the current University of Washington Campus in 1895. It's a beautiful example of the French Renaissance Revival style that stands apart from much of the rest of the University's Collegiate Gothic style. Sit on a nearby bench and imagine what it was like to see this building standing alone 130 years ago.

247 BALLARD CARNEGIE LIBRARY

## 247 BALLARD CARNEGIE LIBRARY

2026 NW Market St
Ballard ⑤

Carnegie grants built 1689 libraries across the U.S. and more than 30 still stand in Washington state. This particular building doesn't serve as a library anymore, but it's still fun to pop into Kangaroo & Kiwi, the Australian and New Zealand-themed bar that occupies the first floor.

## 248 WARD HOUSE

520 E Denny Way
Capitol Hill ③
historicseattle.org/
project/ward-house

This 'residential Victorian carpenter Gothic' home on Capitol Hill is one of the oldest structures in the city of Seattle. It was built in 1882, though it has moved locations since its original build.

## 249 THE ALKI HOMESTEAD

2717 61st Avenue SW
Alki ⑧

Originally known as The Fir Lodge, this building was erected in 1904 as a residence and transitioned to a restaurant in the 1950s. A fire in 2009 put the building at risk of being lost forever, but thankfully it's been refurbished and is now the home of Il Nido, a spectacular Italian restaurant worth visiting.

## 250 FIRE STATION NO. 6

101 23rd Avenue S
Central District ③
+1 206 746 9378
williamgrose.org

The William Grose Center for Cultural Innovation, which opened its doors in summer 2022, is housed in this historic Fire Station in Seattle's Central District. Preservation of the fire station has been a community effort for a decade, as gentrification has threatened this historically Black neighborhood in Seattle. The center is focused on engaging, empowering, and uplifting Seattle's Black community.

# 5 BRIDGES

## *to walk (or ride) across*

### 251 FREEWAY PARK

700 Seneca St
Downtown ②
+1 206 684 4075
seattle.gov/parks/find/
parks/freeway-park

Freeway Park is the best way for you to transit between downtown Seattle and Capitol Hill, avoiding some of the hustle and bustle of traffic lights. You'll cross over the I-5 without even realizing it as you pass through the concrete and foliage-filled park that offers easy access to the Seattle Convention Center. This park was the first of its kind to be built over a freeway in 1976.

### 252 BALLARD (HIRAM M. CHITTENDEN) LOCKS

3015 NW 54th St
Ballard ⑤
+1 206 783 7059
ballardlocks.org

The Hiram M. Chittenden Locks, known to most in Seattle as the Ballard Locks, are both an engineering and environmental marvel. The locks lift boats up or down as they transit from Lake Union to Puget Sound or vice versa. The construction of these locks was part of an enormous reroute of waterways in the City of Seattle, worth exploring further on site or at the Museum of History and Industry.

## 253 MONTLAKE BRIDGE

Montlake
Boulevard E
Montlake ③

The Montlake Bridge spans the Lake Washington ship canal and connects the University of Washington to the Montlake and Capitol Hill neighborhoods. This drawbridge opened in 1925 and opens for four minutes at a time on average to permit boat traffic in the canal below. It's a fun bridge to walk across to view boats passing below on a sunny day. The University of Washington light rail station nearby offers easy access to it.

## 254 EVERGREEN POINT FLOATING BRIDGE

Highway 520
Montlake ③

This current version of this magnificent floating bridge was completed in 2017 and is the longest floating bridge in the world. This latest version offers a multi-use bike and pedestrian path alongside. Drivers, bikers and walkers will enjoy heading west on this bridge particularly on a nice day when the Seattle Skyline, Olympic Mountains are all showing off (for passengers of course, keep your eyes on the road, drivers!)

## 255 LAKE UNION PARK BRIDGE

Lake Union Park 860
Terry Avenue N
South Lake Union ①

Lake Union Park takes up a large portion of the south shores of Lake Union and is filled with bikers, walkers and sunbathers in the good weather days of Seattle's summer. The Lake Union Bridge, recently restored (after much delay!) is a frequent jumping-off point for brave swimmers looking to cool down on the hottest days. In the winter, this bridge provides great birdwatching, for ducks in particular.

## 5 iconic
# SEATTLE LANDMARKS

### 256 CENTER FOR WOODEN BOATS

1010 Valley St
South Lake Union ①
+1 206 382 2628
cwb.org

The Center for Wooden Boats began as a family's collection of historical wooden boats, first open to visitors for viewing in 1976 and becoming a nonprofit in 1979. The structures floating on Lake Union are designated as historic landmarks by the city of Seattle. Don't just walk around the property: rent a wooden boat yourself or attend one of their locally loved Public Sail days, where you'll be guided around Lake Union by a volunteer skipper.

### 257 SMITH TOWER

506 2nd Avenue
Pioneer Square ②
+1 206 624 0414
smithtower.com

The Smith Tower opened to the public in 1914 and was the tallest building in the United States west of the Mississippi River until 1931. The architects who designed the building had previously never designed a building more than five stories tall. The building has been revitalized since a renovation in 2016, though one of the Otis elevators still in operation is still powered by its original DC motor.

260 PIONEER SQUARE TOTEM POLE

## 258 SPACE NEEDLE

400 Broad St
Seattle Center ①
+1 206 905 2100
*spaceneedle.com*

One of the most iconic landmarks in any American city, the Space Needle opened,on the first day of the 1962 World's Fair in Seattle. Improvements made to the structure in 2017 allow for more viewing from multiple glass-enclosed areas. This highlight popular tourist attraction is best enjoyed in early morning (if it's clear) when crowds are light. Alternatively, you can join the crowds for sunset and buy a drink from one of the bars on the lower level.

## 259 KLONDIKE GOLD RUSH NATIONAL HISTORICAL PARK

319 2nd Avenue S
Pioneer Square ②
+1 206 220 4240
*nps.gov/klse*

Seattle as a major metropolitan city exists as it does today because of the Klondike Gold Rush of the end of the 19th century. This National Historical Park in Pioneer Square allows visitors to learn a great deal about the circumstances and all manner of participants in that gold rush and the role Seattle played as a stopover while travelers were en route.

## 260 PIONEER SQUARE TOTEM POLE

100 Yesler Way
Pioneer Square ②

This historic Totem Pole was originally carved in 1790 in a Tlingit village in Alaska in honor of a woman named Chief-of-All-Women. The totem was stolen by a group of Seattle businessmen while they were on a tour of Southeastern Alaska and brought back to Seattle. The totem was damaged in a fire in 1938, but replaced with (the still standing) replica that was carved by descendants of those who worked on the original totem.

# 5 interesting architecture and building **T O U R S**

261 **SEATTLE ARCHITECTURE FOUNDATION**
Various locations
+1 206 667 9184
*seattlearchitecture.org*

Volunteers for the Seattle Architecture Foundation are incredibly knowledgeable and act as excellent tour guides for the multiple offerings from the organization. Downtown tours include (but are not limited to) 'From Stone to Steel: Seattle Style from Then 'til Now' and 'Diamonds & Gold: The Art Deco Skyscraper Northwest Style.' They even have one tour offering to help you find hidden public spaces.

262 **STIMSON-GREEN MANSION**
1204 Minor Avenue
First Hill ③
+1 206 624 9449
*preservewa.org/info/ stimson-green-mansion*

The Stimson-Green Mansion in the First Hill neighborhood is owned and stewarded by the Washington Trust for Historic Preservation. This mansion was completed in 1901 and primarily showcases Tudor and Gothic styles, though you can see a number of other influences. Public tours are offered monthly and are a great way to learn more from the experts about why this is such a special building in Seattle.

### 263 BULLITT CENTER

1501 E Madison St
Capitol Hill ③
bullittcenter.org/
home/tour

The Bullitt Center boasts being 'the greenest commercial building in the world.' You could spend an entire day on their website learning about the various components of this unique building, including its rainwater harvesting, solar panels and gray water system. The University of Washington Center for Integrated Design (CID) offers tours for the public weekly.

### 264 GEOCACHING HQ

837 N 34th St,
Suite 300
Fremont ⑤
+1 206 302 7721
geocachinghq.com/
schedule

If you are already into Geocaching, we probably don't need to tell you that the headquarters of this company are located in Seattle. If you aren't already into Geocaching, there's no better time to start than with a visit to their HQ to cache-in on the GCK25B HQ geocache and exclusive merchandise. The company also sponsors an online tour to help you get to know their surrounding Fremont neighborhood.

### 265 THEATRE TOURS

Various locations
+1 206 682 1414
stgpresents.org/
theatres/tours

The Seattle Theatre Group (STG) operates three of Seattle's best theaters: The Paramount, The Moore and The Neptune. Each of the three historic theaters is open to the public once a month for a free tour with STG. We'd recommend the tour of The Paramount, which originally opened to the public in 1928 and was fully restored back to its original glory in 1995.

# 5 QUIRKY
## *buildings & structures*

### 266 SEATTLE PUBLIC LIBRARY: CENTRAL LIBRARY

1000 4th Avenue
Downtown ②
+1 206 386 4636
spl.org/hours-and-locations/central-library

The City of Seattle's Central Library is a testament to both the simplicity and beauty of glass and steel. It opened in 2004 and was designed by Dutch architect Rem Koolhaas in a joint venture with Seattle-based LMN Architects. While the interior can feel a little maze-like sometimes, the reading spaces and gathering spaces are large and airy.

### 267 WATERFALL GARDEN PARK

219 2nd Avenue S
Pioneer Square ②
pioneersquare.org/experiences/waterfall-garden-park

This 22-foot-high man-made waterfall park will make you feel miles away from the hubub of Pioneer Square. Waterfall Garden Park is open daily during daylight hours and is a great place to bring a take-out lunch or afternoon coffee from a spot nearby.

### 268 THE SPHERES

2111 7th Avenue
Belltown ①
seattlespheres.com

This office building is home to more than 40.000 plants native to 30 different countries. The first tree, an Australian Tree Fern, was planted in 2017. Unfortunately they're only open to the public on the first and third Saturday of the month, by reservation only.

## 269 MOPOP MUSEUM

325 5th Avenue N
Seattle Center ①
+1 206 770 2700
mopop.org

This building is the first commercial architecture project of famed architect Frank O. Ghery designed in the Northwest. The building comprises 3000 stainless steel and aluminum shingles, designed to look different from every viewing angle inspired by the variety and changeability of music itself.

## 270 HAT N' BOOTS

6427 Carleton
Avenue S
Georgetown ⑨
+1 206 684 4075
seattle.gov/parks/find/
parks/oxbow-park

Originally designed for a Western-themed gas station in the 50s, they were saved by local Georgetown residents and relocated to this park in the early 2000s. The cowboy hat has a 44-feet-wide brim and the cowboy boots are more than 20-feet tall.

267 WATERFALL GARDEN PARK

# 35 PLACES TO DISCOVER SEATTLE

———

The 5 best **BEACHES** —————————— 158

5 great **VIEWPOINTS** in Seattle —————— 160

5 scenic **WALKS** ———————————— 163

5 **GARDENS** for springtime blooms ————— 165

5 spots for **FALL FUN** ———————— 168

5 places to discover **SEATTLE'S HISTORY** ——— 170

5 places to find **DARK SEASON JOY** ————— 172

# The 5 best **BEACHES**

## 271 **ALKI BEACH**

2701 Alki Avenue SW
Alki ⑧
+1 206 684 4075
seattle.gov/parks/
allparks/alki-beach-park

Alki is Seattle's slice of Southern California. On a really warm summer day, you might even feel like you're not in the Pacific Northwest, especially when the beach volleyball courts are packed and people are actually swimming (Puget Sound stays quite cold year-round, so most locals only dip on our hottest summer days.) But this beach is beautiful in every season!

271 ALKI BEACH

## 272 GOLDEN GARDENS

8498 Seaview
Place NW
Ballard ⑤
+1 206 684 4075
seattle.gov/parks/
find/parks/golden-
gardens-park

Golden Gardens is a great beach to visit any time of year, though of course it's most popular in summer. The parking lot gets packed on a hot day. Consider visiting in the off season, too. On a windy fall day you'll be entertained by wind surfers and winter views are clearest.

## 273 MADISON PARK BEACH

1900 43rd Avenue E
Madison Park ③
+1 206 684 4075
seattle.gov/parks/
allparks/madison-park

There's not too much sand to share at Madison Park Beach, but locals make the most of this grassy park on nice days all summer long. This east-facing beach has lifeguards in the summer and the lake-front location means slightly warmer water (than the frigid Puget Sound).

## 274 JETTY ISLAND PARK

Everett
+1 425 257 8304
visiteverett.com/1323/
your-guide-to-everetts-
jetty-island

This human-made island acts as a break-water for the city of Everett's Marina, roughly 30 miles north of Seattle. This two-mile long island has no electricity or running water, so pack your bags accordingly for a day of sandy beach fun.

## 275 LOWMAN PARK BEACH

7017 Beach Drive SW
West Seattle ⑧
+1 206 684 4075
seattle.gov/parks/
find/parks/lowman-
beach-park

This small beach in West Seattle has rocky water access and tons of driftwood to sit on and admire the views of Vashon Island, the Olympic Mountains and Puget Sound. Hand carry boat launch is possible on the entire shoreline, though parking can get a little tight on a nice day. It's full of local residents enjoying themselves, especially at sunset.

# 5 great **VIEWPOINTS**
## *in Seattle*

---

### 276 **KERRY PARK**

211 W Highland
Drive
Queen Anne ④
+1 206 684 4075
*seattle.gov/parks/find/*
*parks/kerry-park*

This iconic viewpoint is best when
Mount Rainier is visible seemingly right
behind the downtown skyline. Check
@isthemountainout on twitter to ensure
the ideal photo op! Don't forget to walk
west on Highland Drive to Parsons Garden
and the Betty Bowen viewpoint.

### 277 **GAS WORKS PARK**

2101 N Northlake Way
Northlake ⑤
+1 206 684 4075
*seattle.gov/parks/find/*
*parks/gas-works-park*

Bike or walk along the Burke Gilman trail
from University of Washington (West) or
Fremont (East) to this grassy oasis on the
north shore of Lake Union. Enjoy watching
Seattle's unique seaplanes land on their
aquatic runway and keep an eye out for
live-action-role-players in the fields nearby.

### 278 **THE ROOFTOP BOARDWALK AT T-MOBILE PARK**

1250 1st Avenue S
SoDo ②⑨
+1 206 346 4000
*seattle.mariners.mlb.*
*com/sea/ballpark*

If you're at T-Mobile Park for a Mariners
game or other event, check out the
Rooftop Boardwalk on the highest, west
stadium deck. It's an especially scenic
spot for a seventh-inning stretch to
catch the sunset behind the Olympic
Mountains. Seats in section 318 also enjoy
Seattle skyline views while you enjoy
a baseball game.

### 279 WEST SEATTLE WATER TAXI

Pier 50 Seattle Dock
Downtown ②
+1 206 477 3979
kingcounty.gov/depts/
transportation/water-
taxi.aspx

Hop on the West Seattle Water Taxi for a short and spectacular scenic boat ride. Keep your eyes open for water birds, seals and even the occasional orca. Once in West Seattle, walk North on Alki Avenue to soak in more skyline views or take the free bus connection to explore the Junction or Alki areas.

### 280 DRUMHELLER FOUNTAIN

W Stevens Way NE
UDistrict ⑥
washington.edu

The view of Mount Rainier from Drumheller Fountain can make even the most stressed University of Washington student stop and pause. Situated on Rainier Vista, just southeast of the central campus plaza, the fountain is especially charming in springtime when families of ducks parade their young around.

279 WEST SEATTLE WATER TAXI

281 **OLYMPIC SCULPTURE GARDEN**

281 **ELLIOTT BAY PARK**

# 5 scenic WALKS

## 281 OLYMPIC SCULPTURE GARDEN TO ELLIOTT BAY PARK

Alaskan Way Pier 70
Belltown ①

Starting at the Olympic Sculpture Garden in Belltown, walk North along the Elliott Bay Trail. You'll pass by small beaches, a petite rose garden, offshore salmon pens and a granary ship terminal while enjoying spectacular views of Puget Sound & the Olympic Mountains. Whenever you turn around you'll be greeted by a view of Mount Rainier and the downtown skyline.

## 282 GREEN LAKE LOOP

7201 East Green Lake Drive N
Green Lake ⑤

Come to Green Lake on a nice Seattle day and you'll certainly enjoy yourself. But come on a *rainy* day and really feel like a local, walking the 3-mile loop alongside every kind of Seattleite (and their dogs, strollers and rollerblades). There are a number of bathrooms around the length of the walk and plenty of places for snacks and drinks too, primarily on the east side.

### 283 BALLARD LOCKS TO GOLDEN GARDENS VIA SEAVIEW AVENUE

3015 NW 54th St
Ballard ⑤

After exploring the Ballard Locks, turn west along NW 54th Street, which becomes Seaview Avenue and walk to Golden Gardens Park. On this flat 2-mile walk (one way), you'll pass a number of sweet viewpoint parks, beach access locations and great views of Puget Sound. Look out for kingfishers and cormorants diving for fish at Shilshole Bay Marina.

### 284 MOUNT BAKER BOULEVARD TO MOUNT BAKER BEACH

2957 S Mount
Baker Boulevard
Mt. Baker ⑨

Start this neighborhood walk near Franklin High School and walk up Mount Baker Boulevard, through Mount Baker Park to Mount Baker Beach on Lake Washington. Plenty of trees shade Mount Baker Boulevard as you admire some of the lovely Northwest houses along this road. You can continue your journey along the lake in either direction.

### 285 MADISON STREET

Madison St &
Alaskan Way
Downtown ②

Madison Street is the only street in Seattle that stretches directly from Puget Sound to Lake Washington, and walking it all in one go is both a great workout and a great way to see a lot of the city's variety all at once. It's around 4 miles one way (with quite a bit of elevation gain) and an infinite number of places to stop for food & drink.

# 5 GARDENS
## *for springtime blooms*

---

### 286 SEATTLE JAPANESE GARDEN

1075 Lake
Washington
Boulevard E
Arboretum ③
+1 206 684 4725
*seattlejapanese
garden.org*

Seattle's Japanese Garden offers 3.5 acres of peace and quiet just Northeast of the city center. Each season offers something different to appreciate, but springtime stands out with azaleas, camellias and cherry blossoms with pops of pink at many turns. It's worth visiting midday for the free garden tours available most days at 12.30 pm.

### 287 KUBOTA GARDEN

9817 55th Avenue S
Rainier Beach ⑨
+1 206 725 5060
*kubotagarden.org*

Kubota Garden was originally a privately held property with an owner passionate about horticulture. The garden was saved from development in the 1980s and since then has been managed by Seattle Parks & Recreation and the Kubota Garden Foundation. Parking and visiting the garden is free. Visiting on a weekday offers incredible serenity and calm.

## 288 WASHINGTON PARK ARBORETUM

2300 Arboretum
Drive E
Arboretum ③
+1 206 543 8800
*botanicgardens.*
*uw.edu/washington-*
*park-arboretum*

The 230 acres of the Washington Park
Arboretum are wonderful to visit
any time of year, but springtime is
particularly special with so many trees
and flowers in full bloom. Azalea Way and
the Rhododendron Glen are particularly
vibrant and worth a springtime
stroll. You'll be sure to see plenty of
Washington's state flower, the Pacific
rhododendron.

## 289 UNIVERSITY OF WASHINGTON CHERRY BLOSSOMS

Pierce Lane
UDistrict ⑥
+1 206 543 9198
*washington.edu/*
*cherryblossoms*

The University of Washington's campus
is always worth a visit, especially for its
Collegiate Gothic architecture, but it's
an extra special place for a few weeks
between mid-March and early-April when
the 29 Yoshino cherry trees in the quad
reach peak bloom. The trees are almost
90 years old and transplanted at UW from
the Arboretum in 1964.

## 290 SKAGIT VALLEY TULIP FESTIVAL

311 W Kincaid St
Skagit Valley
+1 360 428 5959
*tulipfestival.org*

While the exact timing of the tulip
festival can vary from year to year due
to weather conditions, the spectacle of
this amazing festival approximately an
hour and a half north of Seattle never
changes. And it's not just about the tulips
(and daffodils!), there are plenty of special
events, including a 4H fair and various
celebrations in nearby Mount Vernon.

290 SKAGIT VALLEY TULIP FESTIVAL

# 5 spots for
# FALL FUN

---

## 291 GEORGETOWN MORGUE

5000 E Marginal
Way S
Georgetown ⑨
+1 206 762 2067
*seattlehaunts.com*

The Georgetown Morgue has gone
through several ownership changes
since its building in 1928, but its original
purpose as place for preparation of the
deceased inspires the current haunted
house it is today. Those interested in
visiting outside of the Halloween high
season can participate in one of their
'escape experiences' – likely to leave you
haunted any time of year.

## 292 NIGHTFALL ORPHANAGE

4544 5st Place
West Seattle ⑧
*nightfallorphanage.com*

This family-run haunted house is at a
private home, so we'll ask that you head
to their website in the fall for updated
visitor information. But once you
arrive, you won't believe you aren't at
an amusement park (probably because
the creators used to work at one).
The organizers usually ask visitors to
donate to a local nonprofit in lieu of any
admission fee.

## 293 LARCH-MARCHING

Various locations in
the East Cascades

While fall arrives earlier in the mountains than it does in Seattle proper, it's worth packing a few extra layers in late September for a hike to view the fall foliage of western and Subalpine larches. Larches are deciduous pine trees, meaning their green pine needles turn a bright yellow each fall, and they are located mostly on the east side of the Cascade Mountain Range.

## 294 FREMONT OKTOBERFEST

Fremont
+1 206 395 4223
fremontoktoberfest.com

Fremont Oktoberfest throws a giant party with dozens of German (and German-inspired) beers to enjoy as summer comes to a close. A great way to experience the festival is as a volunteer, passing out drink tokens or distributing materials to guests, and then getting free entry after your 'hard work' shift is over to enjoy the festivities for yourself.

## 295 WASHINGTON STATE FAIR

110 9th Avenue SW
Puyallup
+1 253 845 1771
thefair.com

The Washington State Fair runs for almost all of each September down in Puyallup, approximately 30 miles south of the city. It's the largest fair in the Northwest and boasts entertainment for all. A few great exhibits not to miss include the Washington State Photographers exhibition and the hobby hall, where local crafters show off their accomplishments.

# *5 places to discover*
# SEATTLE'S HISTORY

296 **BILL SPEIDELS UNDERGROUND TOUR**

614 1st Avenue
Pioneer Square ②
+1 206 682 4646
*undergroundtour.com*

This underground tour is fun for all ages and covers a part of Seattle's history you really have to see to believe. After your visit you'll have a newfound appreciation for the colored glass squares you see along sidewalks throughout Pioneer Square. The tour guides mix humor and history as you stroll up and down sidewalks and stairs hidden from street level.

297 **CHINATOWN DISCOVERY TOURS**

719 S King St
International
District ③
+1 206 623 5124
*wingluke.org/
chinatown-discovery*

The Wing Luke Museum of the Asian Pacific American Experience offers a variety of walking tours to discover the culture, art and history of Asian Pacific Americans in the Northwest. Offerings change seasonally but recent highlights include the Japanese American Remembrance Trail and Bruce Lee's Chinatown. They also offer some spectacular food tours of the International District.

## 298 KLONDIKE GOLD RUSH NATIONAL HISTORICAL PARK

319 2nd Avenue S
Pioneer Square ②
+1 206 220 4240
nps.gov/klse/index.htm

A visit to this National Historical Park is a great compliment to time on the underground tour. Learn more about how the rush to gold in the Yukon Territory of Canada made Seattle what it is today. Rotating exhibits and helpful volunteers make this small park a must-visit for first-time Seattle visitors. Rangers can also help you plan your visits to other parks in Washington.

## 299 TRUE NORTHWEST: THE SEATTLE JOURNEY

AT: MUSEUM OF HISTORY
AND INDUSTRY
860 Terry Avenue N
South Lake Union ①
+1 206 324 1126
mohai.org

The Museum of History and Industry hosts this permanent exhibit on the history of Seattle. The multimedia displays start with early interactions between Native Americans and settlers, Seattle's great fire all the way through modern times. Don't miss the interactive exhibit that shows how the city has been reshaped by digging and damming over the years.

## 300 UNDERWATER DOME

AT: SEATTLE AQUARIUM
1483 Alaskan Way
Pier 59
Downtown ②
+1 206 386 4300
seattleaquarium.org

The Seattle Aquarium takes advantage of sitting on top of the body of water it's working hard to showcase and preserve. The best exhibit is the 400.000-gallon habitat that showcases Puget Sound aquatic life. If you visit Seattle in the summer, keep an eye out for their Beach Naturalists at beaches in the area to learn even more about the surrounding water wildlife.

# *5 places to find*
# DARK SEASON JOY

---

**301 NEON LIGHTS**
  Various locations
  Downtown

Seattle winters are long and dark, but they're made quite a bit brighter thanks to the city's unofficial obsession with neon signs. Make a scavenger hunt out of it and see how many you can photograph, both inside restaurants and bars and out on the city streets. A particularly iconic sign, the Elephant Car Wash, sits at 7th Avenue and Blanchard Street.

301 NEON LIGHTS

## 302 LASER DOME

AT: PACIFIC SCIENCE
CENTER
200 2nd Avenue N
Seattle Center ①
+1 206 443 2001
*pacificsciencecenter.org/*
*visit/laser-dome*

Looking for something fun to do at night but can't find a live concert that strikes your fancy? Check out the schedule for Pacific Science Center's Laser Dome shows. The shows feature music from single artists like Taylor Swift, Cardi B, Pink Floyd, and Daft Punk or more general themes like 'movie magic' alongside spectacular laser light shows.

## 303 NEW YEAR'S DAY BONFIRE

8498 Seaview
Place NW
Ballard ⑤

The first day of the year brings a spectacular bonfire tradition to Golden Gardens Park. Local residents transport their dead and dying Christmas trees to the beach to be lit on fire and entertain participants and observers alike. Bring some hot cocoa and a blanket!.

## 304 ZOO LIGHTS

5500 Phinney
Avenue N
Phinney Ridge ⑤
+1 206 548 2500
*zoo.org*

The Woodland Park Zoo takes advantage of longer nights to offer an incredible light show every winter. All ages will enjoy these wildlife-themed light displays.

## 305 SEATTLE CHRISTMAS BOAT PARADE

Lake Union ①
*seattlechristmas*
*boatparade.com*

While winter may not be high season for boaters in the Pacific Northwest, they do go all-out each December for the annual Christmas Boat Parade on Lake Union. Participants compete for prizes for best in show and other themes, but really the public is just grateful for a chance to admire all the work they put into elaborate light displays.

# 55 WAYS TO ENJOY CULTURE

5 must-explore **MUSEUM EXHIBITS** —————— 176

5 places to learn about
**SEATTLE'S MUSICAL HISTORY** —————— 178

5 **MUSIC** and **PERFORMING ARTS** venues — 180

5 fun things to do at **PIKE PLACE MARKET** — 182

5 local **CULTURAL
AND FOOD FESTIVALS** —————————— 184

5 pieces of cool **PUBLIC ART** ——————— 186

5 **FESTIVALS FOR FILM
AND MUSIC** fans—————————————— 189

5 great **GALLERIES** to explore ——————— 192

5 places to learn about the **NORTHWEST'S
NATIVE INHABITANTS** ————————— 194

5 **CINEMAS** to catch a movie ——————— 196

The 5 best places to **WATCH SPORTS** ——— 198

## 5 must-explore
# MUSEUM EXHIBITS

---

### 306 HOMETOWN DESI
AT: THE WINGLUKE
MUSEUM
**719 S King St**
**International**
**District** ③
**+1 206 623 5124**
*wingluke.org*

The Wing Luke Museum hosts a number of exhibits worth checking out, but the Hometown Desi stands out. The exhibit features stories of South Asian immigrants who came to the Pacific Northwest over the last 100+ years. The exhibit explores how the traditions and cultures these immigrants brought to the PNW have evolved over time and how younger generations relate to being South Asian Americans.

### 307 SCARED TO DEATH: THE THRILL OF HORROR FILM
AT: MOPOP
**325 5th Avenue N**
**Seattle Center** ①
**+1 206 770 2700**
*mopop.org*

Horror movie buffs and even the more casual thriller fans will find something to enjoy at the Museum of Pop Culture's *Scared to Death* exhibit. It features art, costumes and props from a number of famous horror films and spooky television shows. Due to the content included, this exhibit is not recommended for children under 13.

## 308 DEITIES & DEMONS: SUPERNATURAL IN JAPANESE ART

AT: SEATTLE ART MUSEUM

**1300 1st Avenue Downtown ②**

**+1 206 654 3100**

*seattleartmuseum.org*

Head to the Seattle Art Museum for a number of special and permanent art exhibits, but especially for *Deities & Demons*. This exhibit showcases art, sculpture and textiles to help you appreciate the Japanese culture's appreciation of the supernatural. Admission is free on the first Thursday every month, one of many similar offerings at museums around the city.

## 309 NATIONAL NORDIC MUSEUM

**2655 NW Market St Ballard ⑤**

**+1 206 789 5707**

*nordicmuseum.org*

The Nordic Museum in Ballard has existed since 1979, but only recently moved into this glorious newly constructed space. The Museum is dedicated to the history and culture of the entire Nordic region and showcases the influence of Nordic immigrants on life in Seattle and the PNW. It is the largest museum of its kind in the United States.

## 310 CHIHULY GARDEN AND GLASS

**305 Harrison St Seattle Center ①**

**+1 206 753 4940**

*chihulygarden andglass.com*

It's very possible you've come across a Chihuly installation or chandelier in previous travels, as Dale Chihuly is a prolific glass artist. It feels meaningful to view this exhibit not far from the workshop he and his team have occupied on Lake Union for 30 years, which you can read about more in the recently published book *The Boathouse*.

## 5 places to learn about
# SEATTLE'S MUSICAL HISTORY

---

311 **MOPOP: MUSIC EXHIBITS**
    **325 5th Avenue N**
    **Seattle Center** ①
    **+1 206 770 2700**
    *mopop.org/exhibitions-*
    *plus-events/exhibitions/*
    *hendrix-wild-blue-angel*

If you want to better understand Seattle's musical history, start your journey at the Museum of Pop Culture in Seattle Center. Exhibits include deep dives into Nirvana, Jimi Hendrix and hip hop, along with an impressive guitar gallery. Have a young musician or music producer at home? They offer several summer camp options for musically interested youth.

312 **BENAROYA HALL**
    **200 University St**
    **Downtown** ②
    **+1 206 215 4800**
    *seattlesymphony.org/*
    *benaroyahall*

Benaroya Hall is the home of the Seattle Symphony and also hosts performances by artists from all over the globe. The building, which opened in 1998, takes up an entire city block and includes two performing arts halls.

313 **DIMITRIOU'S JAZZ ALLEY**
    **2033 6th Avenue**
    **Belltown** ①
    **+1 206 441 9729**
    *jazzalley.com*

Dimitriou's is 'Seattle's jazz club' and this family-owned establishment has been a fixture of the Seattle music scene since 1980. The unassuming location in Belltown reveals to entrants a classic dinner-show theater setup inside. Top acts from around the country play here six nights a week.

## 314 THE ROYAL ROOM

**5000 Rainier Avenue S**
**Columbia City** ⑨
**+1 206 906 9920**
*theroyalroomseattle.com*

The Royal Room in Columbia City offers live music six nights a week, but that only tells part of its story. The venue also plays home to some exciting and experimental in-house music projects, like The Royal Room Collective Music Ensemble, which is a 15-piece band, and The Piano Starts Here, a project dedicated to great pianists and piano composition.

## 315 LONDON BRIDGE STUDIO

**20021 Ballinger Way NE, Suite A**
**Shoreline**
**+1 206 364 1525**
*londonbridgestudio.com*

London Bridge Studio is located north of Seattle in Shoreline and is famous for hosting the recording of albums from a number of influential artists including Alice in Chains, Pearl Jam and Soundgarden. Fans can sign up to take a one-hour guided tour of the studio, available several days a week for 55 dollars. Advanced booking is required.

313 DIMITRIOU'S JAZZ ALLEY

# 5 MUSIC and PERFORMING ARTS

## venues

---

### 316 PARAMOUNT THEATRE

**911 Pine St**
**Downtown** ②
**+1 206 682 1414**
*stgpresents.org*

Paramount Theatre hosts a wide variety of musical artists, plays and shows, so check the schedule asap for your desired experience. It's the usual place where Broadway shows come to tour and offers a glamorous setting as an excuse to dress up for a night of theater. It's also an enjoyable place to see live music, though the fully seated experience may hinder any folks excited to dance.

316 PARAMOUNT THEATRE

### 317 THE SHOWBOX

**1426 1st Avenue**
**Downtown** ②
**+1 206 628 3151**
*showboxpresents.com*

The Showbox, located directly across from Pike Place Market, is an iconic Seattle music venue that was recently threatened with demolition due to planned development. The art deco venue opened on July 24, 1939 and still retains quite a bit of its original charm. It's been played by greats like Duke Ellington, the Ramones, Pearl Jam.

### 318 TRACTOR TAVERN

**5213 Ballard**
**Avenue NW**
**Ballard** ⑤
**+1 206 789 3599**
*tractortavern.com*

Tractor Tavern is a magical small venue to experience live music. After you've enjoyed dinner or drinks at a nearby Ballard Avenue establishment, head over to see if there are at-the-door tickets available for that night's show, whoever it happens to be. They host a wide range of musical artists from bluegrass, indie pop, rock, jazz and beyond.

### 319 SEA MONSTER LOUNGE

**2202 N 45th St**
**Wallingford** ⑤
**+1 206 355 4247**
*seamonsterlounge.com*

Pretty much every night of the week there is live music at Sea Monster Lounge in Wallingford. Pop in to hear funk, soul, and jazz, and plenty of other genres (live EDM, anyone?). They host local beers on tap and the crowd is always there for a good time. Check their calendar for special events like the occasional Salsa Saturday!

### 320 THE CROCODILE

**2505 1st Avenue**
**Belltown** ①
**+1 206 4206 351**
*thecrocodile.com*

There are some big names that have played The Crocodile over the years for those fans lucky enough to get in at ground level for now-household musicians like Nirvana, R.E.M., Pearl Jam and Macklemore.

# 5 fun things to do at
# PIKE PLACE MARKET

---

### 321 CHEW SOME GUM
AT: GUM WALL
**Post Alley**
**Downtown** ②

Grab a pack of gum on your way to visit Pike Place Market so you can fully participate in arguably one of the city's weirdest traditions. The infamous gum wall is tucked around the corner of Post Alley (the landmark is visible on Google Maps). If you happen to show up and there's no gum on the wall, lucky you! You can be one of the first pieces to restart this fascinating landmark.

### 322 SHOP FOR FLOWERS OR LOCAL CRAFTS
**Various vendors**
**Downtown**
*pikeplacemarket.org/*
*market-directory*

Shopping is really the primary thing to do at Pike Place Market, so it's all a matter of what you're looking to buy. In summer the locally grown dahlias will absolutely bowl you over. Better deals can be found at other markets around the city, but if you're staying in the same place for 5+ days, why not pick up a bouquet? Also keep an eye out for the laser woodwork of Arbor & Hue, which makes a great souvenir or gift.

### 323 WATCH FISH FLY THROUGH THE AIR

**86 Pike Place**
**Downtown** ②
**+1 206 682 7181**
*pikeplacefish.com*

Did you visit Pike Place (or Seattle more generally) if you didn't see a fish flying through the air? The tossing skills of the fishmongers at Pike Place will impress, even if you've managed to catch their prowess on TV or social media before. The extra brave should raise their hand to try and be on the receiving end of one of these fish!

### 324 EAT
AT: PIROSHKY PIROSHKY

**1908 Pike Place**
**Downtown** ②
**+1 206 441 6068**
*piroshkybakery.com*

Options for eating in and around Pike Place Market abound, but one great place to start is Piroshky Piroshky, a locally loved chain offering sweet and savory pastries of Eastern Europe. The owner, Olga Sagan, is a bit of a local celebrity. She opened her first spot in Pike Place in 1992. This location is papered with currency from all over the world, showing that it's not just Seattlites that love these piroshkies.

### 325 LAUGH
AT: UNEXPECTED PRODUCTIONS IMPROV

**1428 Post Alley**
**Downtown** ②
**+1 206 587 2414**
*unexpected productions.org*

After you've had your fill of dinner and drinks near Pike Place, head inside for some laughs at Unexpected Productions Improv. Located adjacent to the Gum Wall in Post Alley, this venue hosts a variety of improv shows 4+ nights a week, sometimes with two shows in one evening. Their Improv Happy Hour shows are a good fit for folks who haven't had much exposure to the genre before.

# 5 local CULTURAL AND FOOD FESTIVALS

## 326 SEAFAIR
**Various locations**
+1 206 728 0123
*seafair.org*

Seafair is usually held on the first weekend of August annually, although related events pop up in the weeks leading up to the festival as well. It's an enormous, city-wide festival that includes boating traditions, a famous airshow and honestly quite a bit of chaos. If you're here the week leading up to the event, you'll likely be amazed by the Blue Angels flying overhead for practice rounds, startling even the most aware visitors.

## 327 BALLARD SEAFOODFEST
**Ballard**
+1 206 784 9705
*seafoodfest.org*

Seattle is a great place to visit if you like seafood, and timing your visit to align with Ballard SeafoodFest means you'll have far too many great options to choose from. The festival, which began in 1974, lasts Friday through Sunday annually on a weekend in July. The festivities shut down a significant portion of Market Street NW and include lots of live music in addition to food vendors and shopping.

## 328 FREMONT SOLSTICE PARADE

**Fremont**
*fremontfair.com/arts/
solstice-parade*

The Fremont Solstice Parade is just one part of the annual Fremont Fair, an enormous celebration of the longest day of the year, art and creativity in the neighborhood of Seattle that calls itself 'the center of the universe.' The parade features community ensembles of all shapes and sizes (and costumes!). For the bold (viewers and participants) the parade is unofficially preceded by an annual naked bike ride hosted by Solstice Cyclists.

## 329 INDIGENOUS PEOPLE FESTIVAL

**305 Harrison St
Seattle Center ①**
*seattlecenter.com/
events/featured-events/
festal/indigenous-
people-festival*

The annual Indigenous People Festival takes place on multiple stages at Seattle Center each June. Performances from local tribes include story times, hoop dancers, flute playing, and spoken word showcases. Several Native vendors nearby will have goods for sale including wearable art, prints and clothing.

## 330 SYTTENDE MAI

**Ballard**
*17thofmay.org*

The 17th of May (Syttende Mai) celebration in Ballard is one of the largest annual celebrations of Norwegian Constitution Day outside of Norway. The first Syttende Mai celebration in Seattle was recorded before Washington was even declared a state. The festivities include events at local businesses, the Leif Erikson Lodge and a parade throughout Ballard. This is a do-not-miss event if you happen to be nearby!

# 5 pieces of cool
# PUBLIC ART

---

331 *ECHO*
**BY JAUME PLENSA**
**2801 Alaskan Way**
**Belltown** ①
**+1 206 654 3100**
*seattleartmuseum.org/*
*visit/olympic-*
*sculpture-park*

As you approach the Seattle Sculpture Garden from Alaskan Way, you'll catch glimpses of a uniquely shaped head staring out at the water and mountains ahead of you. *ECHO* by Jaume Plensa is a 46-feet-tall sculpture that welcomes passers-by to the sculpture garden. It's impossible for this structure not to invite contemplation, as it looks different from every angle.

332 *THE TROLL*
**BY STEVE BADANES**
**& TEAM**
**N 36th St**
**Fremont** ⑤
**+1 206 632 1500**

Tens of thousands of commuters and travelers pass over the Aurora bridge on a daily basis, rarely giving thought to the spooky troll that lurks right beneath the northern end of the bridge. Cemented in pop culture thanks to the film *10 Things I Hate About You*, the troll was constructed in 1990. It is 18 feet tall and clutching a Volkswagen Beetle.

331 *ECHO* BY JAUME PLENSA

332 *THE TROLL* BY STEVE BADANES & TEAM

### 333 *BLACK SUN BY ISAMU NOGUCHI*

**1247 15th Avenue E
Capitol Hill ③
noguchi.org/artworks/
public-works**

A walk around Volunteer Park isn't complete without a short stop to contemplate *Black Sun* by Isamu Noguchi, located directly across the parking lot from the Seattle Asian Art Museum (another great visit if you have the time). This is one of two public pieces of Noguchi's art that you can view in the city of Seattle. This piece was commissioned by the National Endowment for the Arts and installed in 1969.

### 334 *HAMMERING MAN BY JONATHAN BOROFSKY*

**1300 1st Avenue
Downtown ②
+1 206 654 3100
seattlearts.emuseum.
com/objects/2278/
hammering-man**

You can't miss this giant sculpture standing outside of the Seattle Art Museum. At almost 50 feet tall, it's almost impossible to get the whole thing in photo! There are two larger installations of the same name in Frankfurt and Seoul, with several other smaller versions in the U.S. and European cities. Sculptor Jonathan Borofsky says 'the *Hammering Man* celebrates the worker.'

### 335 *WAITING FOR THE INTERURBAN BY RICHARD BEYER*

**601 N 34th St
Fremont ⑤
seattlearts.emuseum.com/
objects/2649/people-
waiting-for-the-
interurban**

This iconic 1979 sculpture is one of the symbols of the Fremont neighborhood. Locals lovingly decorate the sculpture on a seasonal basis, with umbrellas and hats for rainy winters and flowers and rainbow flags in the height of summer. The statue is on the site of the former Seattle to Everett Interurban railroad station. Take a close look at the dog's face for a bit of a surprise.

# 5 FESTIVALS FOR FILM AND MUSIC *fans*

## 336 SEATTLE INTERNATIONAL FILM FESTIVAL

**Various locations**
**+1 206 464 5830**
*siff.net*

The Seattle International Film Festival (SIFF) takes place annually in May and offers the chance for Seattleites and visitors to gather and celebrate films from all over the globe. SIFF as an organization operates soon-to-be five theaters in the city, which include the reopening of the famed Cinerama theater in Belltown in late 2023.

## 337 BUMBERSHOOT

**Seattle Center** ①
*bumbershoot.com*

2023 is a big year for Bumbershoot, as its new owners commit to re-localizing the festival and grounding it in performance art of all kinds. Acts will include a 'cat circus,' sculptures, pole dancers and sign spinners in addition to live music and more well-known forms of art. This music and art festival has a long history in Seattle, taking over Seattle Center each Labor Day (the first weekend in September).

339 **NORTHWEST FOLKLIFE FESTIVAL**

## 338 SEATTLE QUEER FILM FESTIVAL

**Capitol Hill**
**+1 206 323 4274**
*threedollarbill*
*cinema.org/*
*seaqueerfilmfest*

The Seattle Queer Film Festival has been an anchor for the city's queer community since it started in 1996 and continues to be one of the largest of its kind in the region. The festival runs annually each October, and includes opportunities to participate both through in person and virtual screenings, as well as a variety of special events. Films are hosted at theaters downtown, on Capitol Hill and in Columbia City.

## 339 NORTHWEST FOLKLIFE FESTIVAL

**Seattle Center ⓘ**
**+1 206 684 4189**
*nwfolklife.org*

If the weather on Memorial Day Weekend happens to be halfway decent, the Folklife Festival is where you want to be spending your time. It's a free festival in Seattle Center that hosts a wide array of musical acts (both on stage and busking around every corner) as well as artisans with goods for sale. Snag a bite from one of the dozens of food trucks, buy a beer in one of the beer gardens, plop down on the grass and enjoy the music floating towards you from every direction.

## 340 CAPITOL HILL BLOCK PARTY

**Capitol Hill**
*capitolhill*
*blockparty.com*

At Capitol Hill Block Party pretty much any kind of music goes, but acts that make people dance always draw the biggest crowds. The festival turns the busiest part of Capitol Hill into an even wilder mob scene, but if the sun is shining, and you're up for dancing around other people, you'll be sure to have a good time.

# 5 great GALLERIES
## to explore

---

### 341 HENRY ART GALLERY

**15th Avenue NE
& NE 41st St
UDistrict** ⑥
**+1 206 543 2280**
*henryart.org*

The Henry Art Gallery is located on the edge of the University of Washington campus. The museum, which was Seattle's first art museum, was founded in 1926 to showcase contemporary art, which it still focuses on today. The permanent collection contains more than 28.000 objects from all over the world. Exhibits rotate regularly and admission is on a suggested donation basis.

### 342 MICHAEL BIRAWER GALLERY

**1003 1st Avenue
Downtown** ②
**+1 206 624 7773**
*michaelbirawer
store.com*

It's impossible to miss this gallery when you're walking 1st Avenue between downtown Seattle and Pioneer Square. Michael Birawer, the U.S.-based artist, uses multiple styles including graffiti, cartooning, painting and illustration to showcase urban centers across the country. Seattle is one of only two galleries to see the wide range of his artwork in person, and affordable prints allow you to bring a copy of this art home with you as a souvenir.

### 343 STONINGTON GALLERY

**125 S Jackson St**
**Pioneer Square** ②
**+1 206 405 4040**
*stoningtongallery.com*

A walk through Stonington Gallery is a great complimentary experience to the nearby Klondike Gold Rush or Underground Tour, offering the chance to see the art of modern First Nations of the Pacific Northwest Coast and Alaska. Sculptures, paintings, pottery and prints are available for purchase in a wide range of prices. The staff are very helpful and can offer deeper context on pieces on display.

### 344 STEINBRUECK NATIVE GALLERY

**2030 Western**
**Avenue**
**Downtown** ②
**+1 206 441 3821**
*steinbruecknative*
*gallery.com*

Stop into Steinbrueck Native Gallery before or after your visit to Pike Place Market and enjoy one of downtown Seattle's best collections of Native Art. They showcase art exclusively from indigenous artists of the Northwest Coast, Alaska and the Arctic. There's a featured artist or exhibit that changes seasonally and their website offers great background information about the styles of different Nations.

### 345 FRYE ART MUSEUM

**704 Terry Avenue**
**First Hill** ③
**+1 206 622 9250**
*fryemuseum.org*

The Frye Art Museum is located just a short steep walk uphill from downtown. The museum showcases art from early 20th century collectors Charles and Emma Frye, primarily late-nineteenth and early-twentieth-century European art. With admission always free, you can pop in for as little time as is convenient without feeling the need to 'get your money's worth.'

## 5 places to learn about the
# NORTHWEST'S NATIVE INHABITANTS

---

346 **DUWAMISH LONGHOUSE AND CULTURAL CENTER**
**4705 W Marginal Way SW**
**West Seattle** ⑧
**+1 206 431 1582**
*duwamishtribe.org*

The Duwamish Tribe is 'the host tribe of Seattle.' Visit *duwamishtribe.org/history* to learn about their history in the region prior to your visit. The Duwamish Longhouse is in West Seattle. Support the tribe and its mission by visiting the Longhouse Store in person or online.

347 **DAYBREAK STAR CULTURAL CENTER**
**5011 Bernie Whitebear Way**
**Magnolia** ④
**+1 206 285 4425**
*unitedindians.org*

The Daybreak Star Cultural Center is located inside Seattle's Discovery Park and is a cultural gathering place for 'Indians of all Tribes.' The facility hosts a permanent collection of Native art, rotating exhibits and a gift shop.

348 **HIBULB CULTURAL CENTER & NATURAL HISTORY PRESERVE**
**6410 23rd Avenue NE Tulalip**
**+1 360 716 2600**
*hibulbculturalcenter.org*

The Hibulb Cultural Center & Natural History Preserve tells the history and traditions of the Tulalip people and is located in Tulalip, approximately 35 miles north of Seattle. The *Power of Words* exhibit at the Center is particularly informative for those unfamiliar with the Point Elliot Treaty and the role literacy and the written word plays in Tulalip lives today.

### 349 S'GᵂI GᵂI ? ALTXᵂ: HOUSE OF WELCOME

**2800 Dogtooth Lane NW**
**Olympia**
**+1 360 867 6718**
*evergreen.edu/longhouse*

The House of Welcome and Cultural Center is 'A Gathering Place for People of all Cultures' and is located at Evergreen State College in Olympia, 70 miles southwest of Seattle. Local tribes worked together with the university to construct the building in 1995. The facility hosts a variety of educational and festival events open to the public.

### 350 NORTHWEST NATIVE ART

AT: THE BURKE MUSEUM
**4303 Memorial Way Northeast**
**UDistrict** ⑥
**+1 206 543 7907**
*burkemuseum.org*

The Burke Museum at the University of Washington is an excellent place to go to deepen your understanding of Seattle and the PNW, especially through their Northwest Native Art exhibit. It includes rotating contemporary and historic art as well as a canoe, totem poles and pieces of Native house structures.

347 DAYBREAK STAR CULTURAL CENTER

# 5 CINEMAS
## *to catch a movie*

---

### 351 ADMIRAL THEATER

**2343 California
Avenue SW
North Admiral** ⑧
**+1 206 938 0360**
*farawayentertainment.
com/historic-admiral*

The Admiral Theater opened in 1942 and still retains some of its original artwork inside, though the building itself dates back to 1919. The seafaring theme stretches from the giant mural to the signage and architecture. This four-screen theater is a favorite among West Seattle locals, and the reasonable concession prices will keep you coming back (even the local beers are fairly priced!).

### 352 ARK LODGE CINEMAS

**4816 Rainier
Avenue S
Columbia City** ⑨
**+1 206 972 4763**
*arklodgecinemas.com*

Ark Lodge Cinema's name pays homage to its building's original function as a Masonic Lodge. This Columbia City theater is another local favorite, though like most small-time theaters across the United States, has struggled to make ends meet over the last decade. It now shows the newest releases at ticket prices you just can't find at the big theaters.

### 353 CENTRAL CINEMA

**1411 21st Avenue**
**Central District** ③
**+1 206 328 3230**
*central-cinema.com*

Central Cinema calls themselves "Seattle's best dinner and a movie experience" and we're not here to argue. They have monthly screenings of cult favorites like *The Room* in addition to a wide variety of films that sometimes follow a theme (a month of Nic Cage movies!) and sometimes don't. They even offer a weekly Family Cartoon Happy Hour that is free!

### 354 GRAND ILLUSION CINEMA

**1403 NE 50th St**
**UDistrict** ⑥
**+1 206 523 3935**
*grandillusioncinema.org*

The Grand Illusion Cinema is Seattle's longest-running independent cinema. They show a very wide range of films, from popular throwbacks like *Twilight*, to kung fu cult favorites and even some recent releases. Its current building has unfortunately been sold, but management seems confident they will find a way to keep operating either in this location or a new one.

### 355 SIFF CINEMA EGYPTIAN

**805 E Pine St**
**Capitol Hill** ③
**+1 206 464 5830**
*siff.net/year-round-cinema/cinema-venues/siff-cinema-egyptian*

If you're interested in independent films, documentaries or international films, be sure to check out one of the Seattle International Film Festival (SIFF) theaters. The Capitol Hill SIFF Cinema Egyptian is our pick for its quirky Egyptian-themed decor and focus on first-run films. The building was originally constructed in 1916 as a Masonic Temple.

# The 5 best places to
# WATCH SPORTS

___

356 **THE GEORGE & DRAGON PUB**

**206 N 36th St
Fremont** ⑤
**+1 206 695 2768**
*theegeorge.com*

Tucked slightly off the main drag in Fremont is Seattle's best establishment for watching soccer (football, sorry!). Come in early on a Saturday to watch die-hard Premier League fans brave the time difference and drink pints of dark beers before many Seattleites have even woken up. Want to watch the World Cup here? Arrive early, really... early.

357 **ROUGH & TUMBLE PUB**

**5309 22nd Avenue NW, Top Floor
Ballard** ⑤
**+1 206 737 7687**
*roughandtumble pub.com*

Seattle's first sports bar dedicated to watching women's sports felt long overdue when it opened in late 2022. The friendly staff will help you find a seat with a view of whatever game you're interested in and you can enjoy classic pub fare while you watch. More than one big game you're trying to catch? Never fear, there are plenty of TVs.

## 358 BUCKLEY'S

**232 1st Avenue W**
**Lower Queen Anne** ①
**+1 206 691 0232**
*buckleyspubs.com*

So many team flags adorn the walls of this bar that it's hard to be sure whose side they're really on. Die-hard fans and casual brunch-watchers alike will enjoy posting up at a table here for wings, pitchers of beer and some light-hearted banter with the opposing side. The proximity to Climate Pledge Arena means large crowds before home games.

## 359 THE DOCK SPORTS BAR & GRILL

**1102 N 34th St**
**Fremont** ⑤
**+1 206 829 8372**
*fremontdock.com*

The Dock is a quintessential American sports bar and a great place to pop into if you're interested in the Seattle sports scene. You'll have a view of multiple TVs regardless of what seat you snag and you'll be surrounded by plenty of fellow Seattle sports fans. The food here is surprisingly good, considering the casual setup and brisk service, especially the breakfast service during 10 am Sunday NFL games.

## 360 ROOKIES SPORTS BAR AND GRILL

**3820 S Ferdinand St**
**Columbia City** ⑨
**+1 206 722 0301**
*rookiesseattle.com*

Rookies is a family-friendly spot in Columbia City serving casual pub fare. They show more soccer than your average American sports pub, even hosting a Seattle Sounders FC supporter group to watch away games. It doesn't have quite the quantity of televisions as some other sports bars on this list, but the family-friendly vibe makes it worth a visit when you have a game to watch with youngins.

# 40 OUTDOOR ADVENTURES

---

5 wonderful WALKS
IN SEATTLE CITY PARKS —————————— 202

5 great HIKES close to the city ——————— 204

5 places to get out ON THE WATER ————— 206

5 great BIRDING spots ——————————— 208

5 SWIMMING spots for hot days ————— 210

5 FISHING spots in and around the city ——— 212

5 great GOLF COURSES
in and around Seattle ———————————— 214

5 BIKE RIDES for all levels ————————— 216

# 5 *wonderful* WALKS IN SEATTLE CITY PARKS

---

## 361 SCHMITZ PRESERVE PARK

5551 SW Admiral Way
West Seattle ⑧
+1 206 684 4075
seattle.gov/parks/
find/parks/schmitz-
preserve-park

There are a number of entrances into Schmitz Preserve Park, but the easiest is just a stone's throw from Alki beach. Within five minutes of walking (uphill, unfortunately) you'll feel as though you've been transported out of the city neighborhood of West Seattle and into a forested area miles away. There's great birding to be done here year-round and plenty of creek exploring for kids and adults alike.

## 362 DISCOVERY PARK LOOP TRAIL

3801 Discovery
Park Boulevard
Magnolia ④
+1 206 684 4075
seattle.gov/parks/find/
parks/discovery-park

Hop on the well-marked Discovery Park Loop Trail from either the south or visitor center parking lots. Head clockwise around the trail, if possible, as it offers more access to the great views when it comes to the bluff section. This loop trail winds through dark forests, more open small meadows and then onto the beautiful bluffs with views of Puget Sound, the Olympic Mountains and, if you know when to look, Mount Rainier.

## 363 LLANDOVER WOODS

Broadview ⑦
seattle.gov/parks/
allparks/llandover-
woods-greenspace

Talk about a hidden secret! Llandover Woods isn't even commonly visited by the most in-the-know locals. It's an urban forest located in the northeastern most edge of Seattle. In this dense forest valley you'll feel completely separate from the surrounding neighborhood, and you're not likely to see many fellow walkers, either!

## 364 CARKEEK PARK

950 NW Carkeek
Park Road
Broadview ⑦
+1 206 684 4075
seattle.gov/parks/find/
parks/carkeek-park

Carkeek Park has a lot to offer families and all kinds of visitors with several miles of wooded trails, a scenic bridge (over train tracks) with access to a short public beach, and a great playground for kids. The creeks in the park are home to native cutthroat trout as well as chum salmon that's released there by locals. It's also home to one of the only two salmon runs still happening in the city of Seattle.

## 365 LAKERIDGE PARK LOOP

10201 Holyoke Way S
Rainier Valley
+1 206 684 4075
seattle.gov/parks/find/
parks/lakeridge-park

Lakeridge Park is on the southeastern most edge of the City of Seattle and offers a wonderful lollipop loop trail that's approximately one mile long. It's a great loop to do with young children who are just learning to stretch their legs or walk for longer periods of time on their own. The canyon of the park faces north which means NW moss is everywhere you look year-round here.

# 5 great **HIKES**
## *close to the city*

### 366 **DIRTY HARRY'S BALCONY**

53150 Grouse
Ridge Road
North Bend
+1 360 825 1631
dnr.wa.gov/about/dnr-
regions-and-districts

Looking to get out of the city for a half a day or less to a hike with some scenic views? Interested in a hike that's short but will still leave you a little winded and sore from a great workout? Check out Dirty Harry's Balcony, just under 40 miles from downtown Seattle. This hike makes a great pairing with other activities in the North Bend or Snoqualmie areas.

366 DIRTY HARRY'S BALCONY

### 367 WALLACE FALLS STATE PARK

14503 Wallace
Lake Road
Gold Bar
+1 360 793 0420
parks.state.wa.us/289/
wallace-falls

Wallace Falls State Park is a great destination in the springtime in the Northwest, when rain and snowmelt fuels the waterfall. The trail is enjoyable even during springtime rains, as there's a lot of forest cover that takes most of the brunt of the precipitation. This hike starts about an hour from Seattle.

### 368 LAKE SERENE & BRIDAL VEIL FALLS

Mount Index
River Road
Gold Bar
+1 206 625 1367
wta.org/go-hiking/
hikes/lake-serene

This hike will give visitors the perfect taste of how great hiking can be in the PNW, though it is not by any means an easy hike. Over the 8-miles round trip, you'll get to see a spectacular 100-foot waterfall (at its best in the springtime when rain and snowmelt aid its flow) and a beautiful alpine lake. Try to hike here on a weekday.

### 369 DOCKTON FOREST

9500 SW Dock
Maury Island
+1 206 477 4527
vashonparks.org/
dockton-park

Take a short ferry ride from Fauntleroy (West Seattle) to Vashon Island for this scenic hike. Construct your own loop of varying mileage, heading counter-clockwise from the Dockton Park Boat Ramp.

### 370 GOLD CREEK TRAIL AT GREEN MOUNTAIN

1398 Gold Creek
Road W
Bremerton
wta.org/go-hiking/
hikes/green-mountain-1

The Gold Creek Trail at Green Mountain is one of the few trails that actually offers a view of the Seattle skyline. Enjoy your journey to the trailhead, which can include a ferry ride if you choose, and take a moment to observe some of the logging efforts you'll see along your hike. The timber industry has played a huge role in the development of the PNW.

## 5 places to get out
# ON THE WATER

### 371 ALKI KAYAK TOURS

1660 Harbor
Avenue SW
West Seattle ⑧
+1 206 935 7669
kayakalki.com

Alki Kayak Tours offers kayak, paddle board, long board and cruiser bike rentals directly adjacent to the West Seattle Water Taxi and Marination Ma Kai. They only allow for advanced reservations (easy to do online) so be sure to plan a little bit ahead to maximize your enjoyment. Hop on a bike and head down to the bustling heart of Alki or head out into Puget Sound on a kayak and enjoy watching the seals pop up to say hello.

### 372 NORTHWEST OUTDOOR CENTER

2100 Westlake
Avenue N, Suite 1
Westlake ④
+1 206 281 9694
nwoc.com

The Northwest Outdoor Center does incredibly good business in the glorious Seattle summer weather, though it can be just as nice to get out on the water in a kayak or on a paddleboard on a gray day when you have to worry less about applying sunscreen. Set a destination (like Gas Works Park, or the houseboats on the east side of the lake) and watch out for the float plane runway in the middle of the lake!

### 373 LAKE UNION HOT TUB BOATS

2401 N Northlake
Way
Northlake ⑤
+1 206 566 3516
*lakeunionhottub*
*boats.com*

This is the perfect water activity for when the weather actually isn't particularly hot! You can be the captain of your very own hot tub boat, fueled by a wood-fired system made in the Netherlands. Enjoy the coziness of a hot tub in the middle of chilly Lake Union while admiring the Space Needle, Gas Works Park and surrounding neighborhoods. Book your trip ahead of time to be sure to get the date and time you desire.

### 374 AGUA VERDE PADDLE CLUB

1307 NE Boat St
UDistrict ⑥
+1 206 632 1862
*aguaverde*
*paddleclub.com*

If you're stationed in Eastlake, Capitol Hill, Wallingford or the University District, Agua Verde will be the easiest way for you to get out onto the water of Lake Union. There you can rent kayaks and stand-up paddle boards and head west into Lake Union or west through the Montlake Cut into Lake Washington. Their rentals are only available on a first-come, first-served basis.

### 375 GREEN LAKE BOATHOUSE & COFFEE SHOP

7351 East Green
Lake Drive N
Green Lake ⑤
+1 206 527 0171
*greenlakeboathouse.com*

If just walking around Green Lake isn't enough (but you're not entirely sure about swimming in it) head to Green Lake Boathouse & Coffee shop to rent a kayak, paddleboard, pedal boat, water bike or row boat to get out onto Green Lake itself. The prices aren't cheap, but the joy of paddling around this wonderful lake is worth it.

# 5 *great*
# **BIRDING** *spots*

### 376 **LINCOLN PARK**

8011 Fauntleroy
Way SW
West Seattle ⑧
+1 206 684 4075
*seattle.gov/parks/find/
parks/lincoln-park*

Lincoln Park has the opportunity to
see a huge variety of PNW birds, given
that it offers both dense forested trails,
edge environments (great for owls) and
waterfront paths perfect for viewing
all kinds of seabirds. Birds spotted here
throughout the year can include ravens,
yellow-rumped warblers, dark-eyed
juncos, surf scoters, American robins and
bald eagles.

### 377 **WETLANDS AT GOLDEN GARDENS**

8498 Seaview
Place NW
Ballard ⑤
+1 206 684 4075
*seattle.gov/parks/
find/parks/golden-
gardens-park*

At the northernmost end of Golden
Gardens Park (at sea level), there's a small
wetland area that has proved to be an
excellent birding location. You can enjoy
a wide variety of ducks bopping around
during their winter stay in the PNW, and in
late spring and summer the surrounding
foliage is full of migrating warblers of all
kinds. There's even occasionally a beaver
doing work in the ponds.

## 378 UNION BAY NATURAL AREA

3501 NE 41st St
UDistrict ⑥
+1 206 543 8616
botanicgardens.uw.
edu/center-for-urban-
horticulture

This is arguably one of the best birding spots in Seattle proper, and you won't be the only person you see walking around with binoculars. This site is directly adjacent to the University of Washington's Center for Urban Horticulture. The University reports that more than 200 species of birds have been cited here. It's a particularly good spot in winter for duck viewing with more than 4 miles of shoreline.

## 379 BILLY FRANK JR. NISQUALLY NATIONAL WILDLIFE REFUGE

100 Brown Farm
Road NE
Olympia
+1 206 684 4075
fws.gov/nisqually

Located between Tacoma and Olympia, this National Wildlife Refuge is a great stop along a drive of the I-5 or a destination in its own right. It hosts four miles of trails, including a gigantic boardwalk that stretches out over the tidal flats and marsh, offering unparalleled views of a wide variety of birds and other wildlife depending on the time of year and time of day.

## 380 BALLARD LOCKS (FISH LADDER)

2930 W Commodore
Way
Ballard ⑤
+1 206 780 2500
ballardlocks.org/fish-
salmon-ladder.html

The Ballard Locks are worth visiting in their own right, to watch the fish hop up and down this man-made ladder, but you'll find extra amusement as a birder watching seagulls, bald eagles and osprey compete for fish as they make their way up the ladder. You'll also notice a number of harbor seals parking themselves near the entrance to the fish ladder, more congestion means a heartier dinner for them.

# 5 **SWIMMING** *spots*
## *for hot days*

---

**381 COLMAN POOL**

8603 Fauntleroy
Way SW
West Seattle ⑧
+1 206 684 7494
*seattle.gov*

This salt water pool nestled in Lincoln Park in West Seattle is a true local gem. Enjoy views of Puget Sound and the Olympic Mountains while you swim. Hours vary so plan ahead.

**382 MATTHEWS BEACH PARK**

5100 NE 93rd St
Wedgwood ⑥
+1 206 684 4075
*seattle.gov*

Located in North Seattle along Lake Washington, Matthews Beach Park is Seattle's largest freshwater swimming beach. The park also offers a playground for kids, public restrooms and makes a great stop off the Burke-Gilman Trail. Lifeguards are present in the height of summer daily.

**383 GEORGETOWN PLAYFIELD SPRAY PARK**

750 S Homer St
Georgetown ⑨
+1 206 684 4075
*seattle.gov*

There are a number of great spray parks and wading pools around the city of Seattle. Check the Parks Department website for the latest hours and schedules. One relatively new spray park sits in Georgetown among their playfield, tennis and handball courts and swings. Kids will enjoy cooling off in the water features after romping about the area.

### 384 LAKE SAMMAMISH STATE PARK

2182 NW
Sammamish Road
Issaquah
+1 425 649 4275
parks.state.wa.us/533/
Lake-Sammamish

Just outside the city of Seattle sits Lake Sammamish, a large freshwater lake that hosts a state park with fun for anyone in your group. Work up a sweat on one of the park's trails and then hop into the (much warmer than Puget Sound!) waters. You can rent non-motorized boats from Issaquah Paddle Sports.

### 385 FOUR SEASONS HOTEL SEATTLE

99 Union St
Downtown ②
+1 206 749 7000
fourseasons.com/
seattle

If you need another reason to be tempted to stay at the Four Seasons in Seattle, take a look at the spectacular infinity pool on the property with some of the best views you can get from downtown Seattle. There isn't a comparable pool experience in the city. If you aren't able to stay on site, sometimes spa services include poolside time, ask when you're making your reservations to be sure.

381 COLMAN POOL

# 5 **FISHING** *spots*
## *in and around the city*

## 386 SEACREST PARK PIER

AT: SEACREST FERRY DOCK
1660 Harbor Ave SW
West Seattle ⑧
wdfw.wa.gov/places-
to-go/fishing-piers/
seacrest-park-pier

Fishing opportunities can be found on the Washington Department of Fish & Wildlife website. Arguably the most accessible public pier in the city is Seacrest Pier. It is the same dock that the West Seattle Water taxi leaves from, so parking in the area can be challenging at times. From late May to February each year this location is best suited for squid jigging.

386 SEACREST PARK PIER

## 387 BITTER LAKE

620 N 130th St
Bitter Lake ⑦

Bitter Lake sits in a residential neighborhood of the same name in North Seattle. It's a good spot for stocked rainbow trout, rock bass, largemouth bass, and brown bullhead.

## 388 GREEN LAKE

7201 East Green
Lake Drive N
Green Lake ⑤
+1 206 684 4075
seattle.gov/parks/find/
parks/green-lake-park

If you thought there wasn't enough to do at Green Lake in Northern Seattle, fishing is another great activity option! With multiple fishing piers and plenty of ways to get motor-free boats into the water, fishers have the opportunity to catch rainbow and brown trout.

## 389 SPOKANE STREET BRIDGE

3500 W Marginal
Way SW
West Seattle ⑧
wdfw.wa.gov/places-
to-go/fishing-piers/
spokane-st-bridge

For those interested in staying in the city but getting off the beaten path, head to the Spokane Street Bridge. Tribal fishing rights may close down public access at certain times of year. Pay attention to signage and read up on the PNW tribes approach to salmon and other fishing to appreciate their focus on conservation of these important species.

## 390 DES MOINES MARINA PIER

22047 Cliff Avenue S
Des Moines

This is a wonderfully scenic 670-foot pier that's worth walking out on even if your goal isn't to catch local fish or squid. There's plenty to entertain the non-anglers in your party while you fish. The nearby marina offers plenty of boats to look at, the Des Moines beach is a good swimming option nearby and Anthony's HomePort restaurant (a local seafood chain) is adjacent to the marina.

# 5 great **GOLF COURSES**
## in and around Seattle

### 391 DRIVING RANGE AT JEFFERSON PARK GOLF COURSE

4101 Beacon
Avenue S
Beacon Hill ⑨
+1 206 762 4513
premiergc.com/
-jefferson-park-
golf-course

This scenic driving range on Beacon Hill can be enjoyed by even the most casual golfers. With 50 'stalls' this double-decker setup offers drivers a great view of the downtown skyline. There's a full pro shop downstairs, and a 'jumbo' bucket of golf balls (150) will only set you back 17 dollars, so this is a great date or family activity on a budget. There's also an adjacent 18-hole course for the more dedicated players.

### 392 THE GOLF CLUB AT NEWCASTLE

15500 Six Penny Lane
Newcastle
+1 425 793 5566
newcastlegolf.com

This golf club is one of the most scenic in the area, with panoramic views of the Cascade Mountains, Lake Washington, Mount Rainier and even the Seattle skyline. Thankfully, these views can be accessed by the public, though tee times can only be booked one week ahead of time. A set of rental clubs is 85 dollars in addition to your tee time. Book online, with the cost varying depending on demand.

## 393 CHAMBERS BAY

6320 Grandview
Drive W
University Place
+1 877 295 4657
chambersbaygolf.com

Chambers Bay is the most famous local golf course, having hosted the 2015 U.S. Open Championship. Located just south of Tacoma, approximately 40 miles south of downtown Seattle, the course is situated alongside Puget Sound and is open to the public. Tee times are harder to come by for non-residents, but not impossible. You can also always drop into the Chambers Bay Grill to enjoy lunch and the views.

## 394 WEST SEATTLE GOLF COURSE

4470 35th Avenue SW
West Seattle ⑧
+1 206 935 5187
premiergc.com/-west-seattle-golf-course

Parts of West Seattle can make visitors feel much farther away from downtown Seattle than they are, and the local golf course is one of them. Nestled in a valley, just 5 miles southwest of downtown, is a lovely little public golf course. Several holes on the back nine have great views of the skyline and Elliott Bay. Rates for tee times and club rentals are very reasonable.

## 395 WASHINGTON NATIONAL GOLF CLUB

14330 SE Husky Way
Auburn
+1 253 333 5000
washington
nationalgolf.com

Golf fans will find the 35-mile drive out to Washington National Golf Club worth it. This scenic course was designed by John Fought and is the home to the University of Washington Men's and Women's Division 1 collegiate golf teams. Tee times are usually more reasonably priced and easier to come by than the other two elite clubs on this list.

# 5 BIKE RIDES
## *for all levels*

### 396 BURKE-GILMAN TRAIL

Ballard to Kenmore
+1 206 684 7583
*seattle.gov/parks/find/parks/burke-gilman-trail*

The Burke-Gilman Trail stretches 18.8 miles from Kenmore at the north edge of Lake Washington all the way (almost) to Golden Gardens Park along Puget Sound in the Ballard neighborhood. There is a missing section between Fremont and Ballard that is the source of much local frustration. We recommend the section between Matthews Park Beach and Gas Works Park as a nice out and back ride for visitors.

### 397 MADISON BEACH TO SEWARD PARK

START AT: SEWARD PARK
5900 Lake Washington Boulevard S
Seward Park

Starting at Seward Park (or near it), head north along Lake Washington Boulevard alongside Lake Washington itself. On this 7-mile ride (one way) you'll pass by a number of small beaches, boat launches, parks and restaurants. If you pause at Leschi Park, look for the giant sequoia (it's well marked on google maps). There are also plenty of places to stop for refreshment along the way.

## 398 THE CHESHIAHUD LOOP AROUND LAKE UNION

851 Terry Avenue N
Lake Union ①
seattle.gov/parks/
allparks/cheshiahud-
lake-union-loop

You can start this route anywhere that's convenient to your home base, but Lake Union Park will likely have a large number of rideshare bikes available for rent. The Cheshiahud Loop is just over six miles but covers multiple neighborhoods and passes by countless pocket parks and beaches. Start your journey heading north along Westlake for the most beginner biker-friendly path as you get comfortable on your ride.

## 399 WEST SEATTLE VIA HARBOR AVENUE

1660 Harbor
Avenue SW
West Seattle ⑧

Rent a bike (or bring your own on the water taxi) from Alki Kayak Tours and head north along Harbor Ave SW. You'll enjoy great views of the skyline, a killer breeze off of Puget Sound, and as you curve past Alki Beach Pier you'll be in view of Alki Beach and all the fun it has to offer.

## 400 DUTHIE HILL MOUNTAIN BIKE PARK

26300 SE Issaquah-
Fall City Road
Issaquah
+1 206 296 0100
kingcounty.gov/
services/parks-
recreation/parks/trails/
backcountry-trails/
duthie-hill.aspx

Duthie Hill Mountain Bike Park is just over 20 miles outside the city center and offers 6 miles of cross-country trails with almost two miles of freeride trails. There are routes suitable for beginning mountain bikers and more advanced riders alike, and those looking to continue their journey can connect their rides to adjacent Grand Ridge Park. Mountain bike rentals available in Seattle at companies like evo in Fremont.

# 25 THINGS TO DO WITH CHILDREN

5 cool **PLAYGROUNDS** *in Seattle* —————— 220

5 kid-friendly **MUSEUMS** —————— 222

5 lovely **STORES** *for kids* —————— 224

5 fun **ACTIVITIES** *with kids* —————— 226

5 great **WALKS** *with kids* —————— 228

# 5 cool
# **PLAYGROUNDS** *in Seattle*

## 401 **WESTCREST PARK**

9000 8th Avenue SW
Highland Park ⑧
+1 206 684 4075
seattle.gov/parks/find/
parks/westcrest-park

Westcrest Park sits on the south edge of Seattle, on a large hill above the Duwamish River valley and west of Boeing Field. The large play area has a great view to the east and north of the city skyline and on a clear day, some of the Cascade Mountain Range. There's a nearby community garden to explore, a few trails to wander and an off-leash dog park for your furry children.

## 402 **LINCOLN PARK**

8011 Fauntleroy
Way SW
West Seattle ⑧
+1 206 684 4075
seattle.gov/parks/find/
parks/lincoln-park

There's something a little bit magical about the north play area at Lincoln Park, nestled among the giant trees of this large West Seattle park. It's shady most of the day, there are restrooms adjacent to the playground and ball fields are a short walk away. Caregivers and kids alike can join peek-a-boo views of the Olympic Mountains through the trees.

## 403 SEATTLE CHILDREN'S PLAYGARDEN

1745 24th Avenue S
Judkins Park ⑨
+1 206 325 5576
childrensplaygarden.org

The PlayGarden is designed for children 'of all abilities to enjoy a safe, accessible, and adventurous play to play.' They offer free play times with supervision in the summer, though the playground is not open at all times as the facility offers a preschool and other special camps and events. The playground meets a great need for children with varying abilities to have access to fun and adventure play in the city.

## 404 SALMON BAY PARK

2001 NW Canoe Place
Ballard ⑤
+1 206 684 4075
seattle.gov/parks/find/
parks/salmon-bay-park

Salmon Bay Park is just a mile or so north of the main shopping and dining part of Ballard in a more residential part of the neighborhood. It's a moderately sized play structure and swing set that is often littered with local children's toys, left behind to be shared with future visitors. The park includes several grassy areas for picnicking as well as bathroom facilities.

## 405 ROXHILL PARK

2850 SW Roxbury St
West Seattle ⑧
+1 206 684 4075
seattle.gov/parks/find/
parks/roxhill-park

Local residents call Roxhill Park the 'Castle Park' for the playground structure that inspires the imaginations of local kids daily. There's also a top-notch skate park, and multiple soccer and baseball fields here, along with several gravel and paved trails that traverse through the wetland area and the headwaters of Longfellow Creek.

# 5 kid-friendly **MUSEUMS**

### 406 **SEATTLE AQUARIUM**

1483 Alaskan Way
Pier 59
Downtown ②
+1 206 386 4300
seattleaquarium.org

The Seattle Aquarium's prime waterfront location, just blocks downhill from Pike Place, makes it a great alternative to outdoor exploration if the weather on your visit isn't cooperating. They recently opened the 'Caring Cove,' an open play space where kids can play-act a variety of animal care activities. Time your visit to line up with one of the daily exhibit talks or mammal feeding times, all listed on their website.

### 407 **SEATTLE CHILDREN'S MUSEUM**

305 Harrison St
Seattle Center ①
+1 206 441 1768
seattlechildrens
museum.org

Conveniently located in the heart of Seattle Center, the Seattle Children's Museum offers a wide array of exploratory play exhibits primarily for kids ten and under. Their *Tribal Tales* exhibit was developed in collaboration with local tribes, and can offer kids (and their parents!) a hand in understanding the long history of Native peoples in Seattle.

### 408 KIDIMU

301 Ravine Lane NE
Bainbridge Island
+1 206 855 4650
kidimu.org

KiDiMu, aka the Kids Discovery Museum, is a short, scenic ferry ride from downtown Seattle on Bainbridge Island. The activities and exhibits here are designed for children from six months to ten years of age. They also offer an *Explore Bainbridge* activities book to help kids and families explore other sites on the island through science, technology, engineering, and math activities.

### 409 WOODLAND PARK ZOO

5500 Phinney
Avenue N
Phinney Ridge ⑤
+1 206 548 2500
zoo.org

Once you're inside the Woodland Park Zoo, you'll feel farther away from downtown than you actually are. While the more exotic animals might draw the attention of kids and adults alike, first time visitors to the PNW should be sure to visit the Living Northwest Trail, designed to help visitors appreciate the wildlife all around our region.

### 410 KIDS FLIGHT ZONE @ MUSEUM OF FLIGHT

9404 E Marginal
Way S
South Seattle ⑨
+1 206 764 5700
museumofflight.org/
exhibits-and-events/
exhibits/kids-flight-zone

Budding pilots and engineers will be enamored with the opportunity to sit inside the cockpits of various aircraft in the Kids Flight Zone. With a number of aircraft on display both inside the museum and out on the tarmac (the museum is adjacent to the King County Airport), there is tons to look at for kids and adults of all ages.

# 5 lovely **STORES**
## *for kids*

---

### 411 SNAPDOODLE TOYS & GAMES

120 N 85th St
Greenwood ⑤
+1 206 782 0098
snapdoodletoys.com

This family-owned toy store has six locations in the Seattle metro area, all focused on unplugged play and learning games and toys for kids of all ages. Their Greenwood location is the largest, with plenty for your kiddo to be excited about. This location also offers The Salon@ Snapdoodle which offers kids haircuts, in case somebody needs a trim.

### 412 MY THREE LITTLE BIRDS

4736 California Avenue SW
The Junction ⑧
+1 206 946 6591
my3littlebirds.com

The My Three Little Birds store in West Seattle offers new and gently used children's clothing and games for kids 12 and under. They restock their consignment section daily, so there's always the possibility of a new great find. They focus on higher quality and mid-range to upscale brands of children's clothing, shoes, gear and toys.

## 413 CLOVER TOYS

4609 14th Avenue
NW, Suite 103
Ballard ⑤
+1 206 782 0715
shopclovertoys.com

Clover Toys in Ballard is a boutique children's toy store. They've been woman-owned since they opened in 2004, though new ownership took over in 2017. They have great gift guides to browse online before your visit for multiple age ranges, though we also recommend heading into the store to get the advice of one of their friendly staff members.

## 414 SUGARLUMP

3107 South Day St
Mt. Baker ⑨
+1 206 860 5083
sugarlumpshop.com

The Sugarlump tagline is 'from bump to big kid!' This Madison Valley consignment boutique has been in the area for 20+ years. They sell maternity and kids clothes, including boys clothing up to size 10/12 and girls clothing sizes from newborn to 14/16. Their focus is on higher-end brands for the discerning parent-to-be and their kids.

## 415 BLUE HIGHWAY GAMES

2203 Queen Anne
Avenue N
Queen Anne ④
+1 206 282 0540
bluehighwaygames.com

Perched at the very top of Queen Anne Hill, Blue Highway Games is a great place to pop into with kids interested in board and card games or puzzles. Their community space is available for public use for game play during their open hours. They have a snack bar for purchasing drinks and snacks to fuel multiple rounds of your next favorite game.

# 5 fun ACTIVITIES
## with kids

### 416 PACIFIC SCIENCE CENTER

200 2nd Avenue N
Seattle Center ①
+1 206 443 2001
pacificsciencecenter.org

The Pacific Science Center, located conveniently among plenty of other attractions in Seattle Center, has a number of exhibits great for kids. The Tinker Tank Makerspace allows kids to get hands-on experience building their own creations while the tropical butterfly house will enamor kids who are excited about animals and the natural world. They also host Seattle's two IMAX theaters and a planetarium.

417 GREEN LAKE PITCH & PUTT

### 417 GREEN LAKE PITCH & PUTT

5701 East Green
Lake Way N
Green Lake ⑤
+1 206 632 2280
greenlakegolfcourse.com

Green Lake Pitch & Putt is a great place to head with older kids who want to try out what it feels like to shoot around a course larger than a mini-golf course, without the commitment of 18 holes. Their nine-hole course is par 3, directly adjacent to Green Lake Park. Clubs are very affordable to rent, and it's first-come, first-served.

### 418 SEATTLE BOULDERING PROJECT

900 Poplar Place S
Central District ③
+1 206 299 2300
seattlebouldering
project.com

Bouldering is a great activity to try with active kids who might enjoy a new challenge. Both their Poplar and Fremont locations have areas specially designed for youth and families. There's no experience necessary to drop in and try things out.

### 419 OUTER SPACE SEATTLE

2820 Alki Avenue SW
Alki ⑧
+1 206 397 4591
outerspaceseattle.com

This space-themed indoor play area is located along the main business strip of Alki Beach in West Seattle. They even offer a 'Kids Night Out!' supervised play night on Fridays from 5.30 to 8.30 pm (advanced registration required) that gives parents the opportunity for a nearby date.

### 420 KIDS INFLATABLE FUN ZONE: ARENA SPORTS MAGNUSON

7751 63rd Avenue NE
Sand Point ⑥
+1 206 985 8990
arenasports.net/
magnuson

Rain or cloudy skies dampening your planned outdoor activities with your young ones? Head to the Inflatable FunZone at Arena Sports in Magnuson Park; it is a huge hit with local kids. Kids ages 18 months to 12-year olds will wear themselves out running and jumping all over this large indoor playground with multiple bounce houses.

# 5 great WALKS
## with kids

### 421 SEWARD PARK OUTER LOOP

5900 Lake
Washington
Boulevard S
Seward Park ⑨
+1 206 684 4396
seattle.gov/parks/find/
parks/seward-park

Seward Park, in South Seattle, is a peninsula surrounded by Lake Washington. There's a playground (with a scenic view of the lake and Mount Rainier) located right next to bathrooms and the Seward Park Audubon Center, which offers regular birding classes and walks. The 2.4-mile paved trail around the perimeter of the park, alongside the lake, is perfect for strollers and kids learning to enjoy the outdoors but perhaps unsteady on their feet.

### 422 JEFFERSON PARK

3801 Beacon Avenue S
Beacon Hill ⑨
+1 206 684 4075
seattle.gov/parks/find/
parks/jefferson-park

Jefferson Park has a wonderful walking path around its perimeter that offers various viewpoints to take in the Duwamish River, Seattle's skyline and the Olympic Mountains. The park also has a skate park, a playground and impressive slide system, and plenty of lawn space to spread out on. It also happens to be adjacent to the Jefferson Park Golf Course & driving range, in case you need even more activity!

### 423 SEAHURST PARK

1600 SW Seahurst
Park Road
Burien
+1 206 988 3700
burienwa.gov/
residents/parks_
recreation_cultural_
services/city_parks_
trails_facilities/
seahurst_park

Seahurst Park is just south of Seattle, in Burien, and it offers wonderful beach access to Puget Sound and views of the Olympic Mountains. They have reservable picnic shelters and tables (great for parties and family gatherings). There are also a number of forested hiking trails that can combine into a sizeable loop, if you have kids up for a longer adventure.

### 424 SEATTLE CENTER

305 Harrison St
Seattle Center ①
seattlecenter.com

Seattle Center, especially in summer, is a real feast for the senses. There's so much to look at and interact with, from food and craft vendors, the Seattle Children's Theatre, the looming Space Needle and so much more! The A highlight for kids is certainly the giant International Fountain, which was constructed in 1962 for the World's Fair and was inspired by outer space exploration.

### 425 VOLUNTEER PARK

1247 15th Avenue E
Capitol Hill ③
seattle.gov/parks/find/
parks/volunteer-park

Adults visiting Volunteer Park might appreciate that it's one of Seattle's historic Olmsted Parks, while younger visitors will enjoy the wading pool on hot days and the large playground near the northeast entrance. Hiking up to the top of the historic water tower is a fun accomplishment for little legs, and there's plenty to learn on the interpretive signage for more mature visitors.

ARCTIC CLUB SEATTLE

# 30 PLACES
# TO SLEEP

---

5 nice **NEIGHBORHOODS**
to rent a place to stay —————————— 232

5 hotels **WITH GREAT VIEWS** —————— 234

5 **BOUTIQUE** hotels —————————— 236

5 of the best **CAMPSITES** near Seattle———— 238

5 great places **OUTSIDE THE CITY** to stay —— 240

5 **SUSTAINABLE** stays ———————— 242

# 5 *nice* **NEIGHBORHOODS**
## *to rent a place to stay*

---

#### 426 **BALLARD**
Ballard ⑤

Do you like beer? If the answer is even remotely yes, rent a spot in Ballard and then you can spend at least one (or two) afternoons bouncing around between the endless variety of breweries within walking distance. Ballard also offers great dining and shopping options, as well as great access to outdoor attractions like Golden Gardens Beach and the Ballard Locks.

#### 427 **CAPITOL HILL**
Capitol Hill ③

If your priorities when traveling are dining and nightlife, Capitol Hill is the neighborhood for you. It's also the queer epicenter of Seattle, with the city's highest concentration of gay bars and nightclubs. If you want easy access to all this fun, but a little less urban grunge in your accommodations, look for a spot in North Capitol Hill, closer to Volunteer Park which will be quieter, but still has easy access to all the fun.

## 428 LOWER QUEEN ANNE

Lower Queen Anne ⓘ

If you are planning to attend any events at Seattle Center or traveling for business in the South Lake Union neighborhood, the Lower Queen Anne neighborhood is a fun place to use as a home base. Be sure to check out the W Thomas Street Pedestrian (and bike) Bridge to access the Elliot Bay trail, especially scenic at sunset.

## 429 BELLTOWN

Belltown ⓘ

Just north of downtown Seattle, Belltown has pockets of slightly calmer city living. With equal distance between the attractions of Pike Place and Seattle Center, Belltown is a great spot to stay for a first time Seattle visitor. Enjoy the bars and restaurants that line First and Second Avenues, as well as the easy access to the Seattle Art Museum's Sculpture Garden along the waterfront.

## 430 COLUMBIA CITY

Columbia City ⑨

Staying in Columbia City offers a totally different perspective on Seattle, perfect if you want to imagine what it would be like to live here year-round. The Columbia City light rail station will offer easy access to all the major attractions (downtown, Capitol Hill and the University of Washington), while you'll also have plenty to explore nearby including great restaurants and nearby Seward Park.

# 5 hotels
# WITH GREAT VIEWS

### 431 THE EDGEWATER HOTEL
2411 Alaskan Way
Belltown ①
+1 206 792 5959
edgewaterhotel.com

The Edgewater Hotel was originally built for the 1962 World's Fair and has hosted a number of famous guests over the years. The Beatles Suite is the actual location where The Beatles fished out of the window in 1964.

### 432 FOUR SEASONS HOTEL SEATTLE
99 Union St
Downtown ②
+1 206 749 7000
fourseasons.com/
seattle

Of course the Four Seasons occupies a spectacular piece of real estate in Seattle. West-facing rooms will deliver the best Elliott Bay and Olympic Mountain views. Can't quite swing a room here? Book a table at the Goldfish to pretend for the evening.

### 433 SEATTLE MARRIOTT WATERFRONT
2100 Alaskan Way
Downtown ②
+1 206 443 5000
marriott.com/en-us/
hotels/seawf-seattle-
marriott-waterfront

This Marriott property offers wonderful views of Elliott Bay, West Seattle and the Olympic Mountains. This is a two-for-one recommendation, though, as another nearby Marriott property, the Courtyard by Marriott Seattle Downtown/Lake Union, also has great Lake Union water views for a slightly lower price point. Both offer great access to downtown Seattle, Seattle Center & South Lake Union.

### 434 THOMPSON SEATTLE

110 Stewart St
Downtown ②
+1 206 623 4600
hyatt.com/thompson-
hotels

This World of Hyatt property is a stylish, pet-friendly option located on the north edge of Downtown. They have 150 rooms, suites and residences, many of which offer spectacular views of Elliott Bay and the surrounding mountains. Their rooftop bar, Nest, is worth visiting even if you aren't staying on the property, for its spectacular views and inventive cocktails.

### 435 GRADUATE SEATTLE

4507 Brooklyn
Avenue NE
UDistrict ⑥
+1 206 634 2000
graduatehotels.com/
seattle

While you're more likely to come across visiting intellectuals than business people at the Graduate, given its proximity to the University of Washington, it's worth considering a stay here to get slightly out of the high tourist zone of the city. The views from the Mountaineer Club, their rooftop bar on the 16th floor, boasts panoramic views of the city and surrounding mountains and bodies of water.

435 GRADUATE SEATTLE

# 5 BOUTIQUE *hotels*

### 436 HOTEL BALLARD

5216 Ballard
Avenue NW
Ballard ⑤
+1 206 789 5012
hotelballardseattle.com

There are shockingly few hotel stays available in the northwest neighborhoods of Seattle, but Hotel Ballard makes up for it by being a stylish, spectacularly located boutique hotel nestled in the heart of the Ballard neighborhood. Guests have access to the upscale Olympic Athletic Club, an in-hotel spa and the attached Stoneburner Restaurant, enjoyed by locals and visitors alike.

### 437 THE INN AT THE MARKET

86 Pine St
Downtown ②
+1 206 443 3600
innatthemarket.com

The name really says it all. The Inn at the Market is the only hotel located directly within Pike Place Market, so if you really want to stay in the thick of things, while still enjoying the amenities of an upscale boutique hotel, this spot is for you. Attached to the hotel is more than one excellent restaurant, including Sushi Kashiba, a top spot for sushi in the city.

## 438 ARCTIC CLUB SEATTLE

700 3rd Avenue
Pioneer Square ②
+1 206 776 9090
arcticclubhotel.com

Stepping into the Arctic Club's lobby and bar makes you feel like you've stepped through time (with the exception of the glowing polar bear in the corner of the hotel bar). The Arctic Club was founded in 1907 by a group of successful participants in the Klondike Gold Rush, and the hotel was later designed in 1916 by A. Warren Gould, one of Seattle's best-known architects of the time.

## 439 THE HEATHMAN HOTEL

220 Kirkland Avenue
Kirkland
+1 425 284 5800
heathmankirkland.com

The Heathman Hotel in Kirkland is located just 10 miles outside of Seattle, a short drive (or public transit ride) to any sights. The Heathman is the only boutique hotel in downtown Kirkland, which has plenty of its own amenities to offer, including a number of great restaurants and bars and a beautiful waterfront to enjoy, especially at sunset.

## 440 HOTEL MAX

620 Stewart St
Downtown ①
+1 206 728 6299
provenancehotels.com/
hotel-max-seattle

Hotel Max's target audience is creators and those with an eye for design, music and culture. This stylish Provenance property offers a variety of room options, including 'mini' rooms for those prioritizing a place to lay their head. They have a number of special amenities for guests, including bike rentals and a craft beer happy hour.

# 5 of the best
# CAMPSITES *near Seattle*

---

### 441 DASH POINT STATE PARK

5700 SW Dash
Point Road
Federal Way
+1 253 661 4955
parks.state.wa.us/496/
dash-point

Located almost equidistant between the cities of Seattle and Tacoma, this spectacular state park makes you feel a world away from those urban centers. With 114 standard campsites, 27 utility campsites and a few rustic cabins available for rental, you can sleep among the pine trees alongside Puget Sound while still being a short drive from urban attractions. The park has 11 miles of hiking trails and a large beach to explore.

### 442 TOLT MACDONALD PARK & CAMPGROUND

31020 NE 40th St
Carnation
+1 206 477 4527
kingcounty.gov/
services/parks-
recreation/parks

Located in the town of Carnation, approximately 30 miles outside the city of Seattle, Told MacDonald Park & Campground is run by King County Parks. If you visit in the fall, keep an eye out for spawning Chinook salmon in the Snoqualmie River (along with the eagles and osprey hunting them from above). There are a number of seasonally available tent campsites, yurts and RV hookups here.

## 443 SALTWATER STATE PARK

25205 8th Place S
Des Moines
+1 253 661 4956
parks.state.wa.us/578/
saltwater

Saltwater State Park is located less than 20 miles south of downtown Seattle and has 35 campsites available for rent year-round. There are a few forested trails inside the park and more than 1400 feet of urban beach to explore. The park also is home to the state's only underwater artificial reef, which is immensely popular with local scuba divers.

## 444 MIDDLE FORK CAMPGROUND

along the NF-5600
North Bed
+1 888 448 1474
recreation.gov/
camping/campgrounds/
234501

Those who enjoy time outside (and if you're reading the camping section, that's likely you) should drive out the Middle Fork Road whether you're interested in camping or not. There are tons of trailheads along the way, including The Gateway Bridge, which is very close to the Middle Fork Campground. This campground is located next to the Middle Fork of the beautiful Snoqualmie River.

## 445 FAY BAINBRIDGE PARK

15446 Sunrise
Drive NE
Bainbridge Island
+1 206 842 3931
biparks.org/fay-
bainbridge-park-
campground

Fay Bainbridge Park is operated by the Bainbridge Island Metro Parks & Recreation District. This 17-acre waterfront park has 17 tent sites and 25 RV sites, most of which can be reserved ahead of time. If you aren't looking to pack your tents for your travels, there are also a few cabins available for rent. Enjoy the sounds of the sea and the views of the Cascade Mountains to the east.

## 5 great places
# OUTSIDE THE CITY
## to stay

---

### 446 TREEHOUSE POINT

6922 Preston-Fall
City Road
Issaquah
+1 425 441 8087
treehousepoint.com

Looking for a truly unique place to stay when you visit the Pacific Northwest? Look no further than Treehouse Point, located approximately 25 miles from downtown Seattle nestled next to Raging River. There are six treehouses to choose from, all available for rent throughout the year when there aren't special events.

### 447 THREE TREE POINT B&B

17026 33rd Avenue SW
Burien
+1 206 669 7646
3treepointbnb.com

This small, family-run bed and breakfast is located roughly 13 miles south of downtown Seattle in the town of Burien. It's the perfect place to stay if you want to experience personal touches and spectacular views of both Mount Rainier and the Olympic Mountains.

### 448 SALISH LODGE & SPA

6501 Railroad
Avenue
Snoqualmie
+1 425 888 2556
salishlodge.com

The Salish Lodge & Spa is located in Snoqualmie, directly adjacent to the magnificent Snoqualmie Falls. Their award-winning spa is a destination for many Seattleites, so why not just stay on the property for easy access? There are countless outdoor experiences just beyond the property as well.

## 449 THE WOODMARK HOTEL & STILL

1200 Carillon Point
Kirkland
+1 425 822 3700
thewoodmark.com

The Woodmark Hotel is perched on the east side of Lake Washington, directly across the lake from the University of Washington with easy access to downtown Bellevue and Kirkland. This luxury resort boasts a wonderful lakeside patio (especially to watch the sun set over the Olympic Mountains). There are four restaurants to choose from on the property as well as a well-regarded spa.

## 450 THE LODGE AT ST. EDWARD

14477 Juanita
Drive NE
Kenmore
+1 425 470 6500
thelodgeatstedward.com

This new hotel sits uniquely inside St. Edward State Park, just south of the city of Kenmore, on the northeast shore of Lake Washington. The building operated as a seminary for 45 years. Today the 84 guest rooms offer unparalleled access to the state park's nearby trails and waterfront access, as well as a lovely on-site bar, restaurant and spa.

448 SALISH LODGE & SPA

# 5 **SUSTAINABLE** *stays*

### 451 **CITIZENM SEATTLE SOUTH LAKE UNION**

201 Westlake
Avenue N
South Lake Union ⓘ
+1 206 336 3525
citizenm.com/hotels/
united-states/seattle/
seattle-south-lake-
union-hotel

This citizenM was a welcome addition to the Seattle scene when it opened in 2020. The stylish lobby, bar, gathering spaces and meeting rooms make it easy to socialize or get work done at any time of day. While many guests are often tech workers traveling, this is also a great location for tourists interested in staying just outside the hubbub of downtown. Rest your head at night knowing the property is LEED Gold Certified.

451 **CITIZENM SEATTLE SOUTH LAKE UNION**

## 452 HYATT AT OLIVE 8

1635 8th Avenue
Downtown ①
+1 206 695 1234
hyatt.com/en-US/
hotel/washington/
hyatt-at-olive-8

The Hyatt at Olive 8's convenient location to both downtown and Capitol Hill attractions is complemented by its LEED Silver status. The hotel also has one of the largest green roofs in downtown (8000+ square feet!), which retains rainwater, insulates indoor spaces and has a chef's garden.

## 453 CEDARBROOK LODGE

18525 36th Avenue S
SeaTac
+1 206 901 9268
cedarbrooklodge.com/
inspire.php

Cedarbrook Lodge is not your typical airport hotel in its amenities, setting or its commitment to sustainability. The four pillars of their approach to sustainability include agricultural stewardship, supply chain integrity, natural resource efficiency and community enrichment. It's just 15 miles south of downtown Seattle.

## 454 FAIRMONT OLYMPIC HOTEL

411 University St
Downtown ②
+1 206 621 1700
fairmont.com/seattle

This luxurious property has been the site of a hotel since the 1920s, and it has hosted numerous special guests over the years, including quite a few American Presidents. Modern day special guests include the honey bees that reside on the rooftop of the hotel.

## 455 HYATT REGENCY SEATTLE

808 Howell St
Downtown ①
+1 206 973 1234
hyatt.com/en-US/
hotel/washington/
hyatt-at-olive-8/seahs

The Hyatt Regency in downtown Seattle opened in late 2018 with great fanfare as the first hotel in the city to be LEED Gold Certified. Sustainability fans will find a number of things to appreciate while staying at this modern hotel, including systems that reduce energy use, water waste and a focus on local food offerings and the reduction of food waste.

# 30 ACTIVITIES FOR WEEKENDS

———

5 superb WEEKEND GETAWAYS ———— 246

5 day trips to EXPLORE THE PNW ———— 248

5 worth-renting-a-car MULTI-DAY HIKES —— 251

5 DAY HIKES worth driving for———— 253

5 places to TRY A NEW HOBBY ———— 256

5 of the best WINTER WEEKENDS ———— 258

## *5 superb*
# WEEKEND GETAWAYS

---

### 456 STEHEKIN
Stehekin, WA

A trip to the tiny 'town' of Stehekin will take some advanced planning, as it's a car-free town that requires a ferry ride (or a 23-mile hike) to get to. All your efforts will be worth it, though, as you enjoy the pristine views and water activities on Lake Chelan, one of the deepest lakes in the United States. Make sure to find time in your visit to pay homage to your sweet tooth at the Stehekin Pastry Company.

456 STEHEKIN

### 457 PORT ANGELES
Port Angeles, WA

Port Angeles is 'the gateway to the Olympic Mountains' and full of fun and quirky restaurants, bars and galleries. Even if you aren't a hiker, drive up to the Hurricane Ridge viewpoint to enjoy some of the best mountain views accessible by car in the state.

### 458 FRIDAY HARBOR
Friday Harbor, WA

Friday Harbor is the main seaport town on San Juan Island, the most populous island in this archipelago between the Washington State mainland and Canada's Vancouver Island. Wildlife watching, particularly for whales, is particularly popular for visitors and locals alike.

### 459 YAKIMA
Yakima, WA

The 'Palm Springs of Washington' is a great escape from cloudy Seattle between March and June. Pack your sneakers to hike the Yakima Skyline Trail for great views or head to Cowiche Canyon where you can even hike to a nearby vineyard. Don't miss Owen Roe or Fortuity for wine tastings!

### 460 WHITE SALMON
White Salmon, WA

This small town located on the Columbia River is a picturesque place to visit and explore the Columbia River Gorge from. Wind sports are particularly popular here and across the river in Hood River, OR. Whether your interests are more inclined towards wine tasting and sightseeing or hiking and kayaking, there's something for everyone within a short drive.

# 5 day trips to
# EXPLORE THE PNW

---

### 461 BAINBRIDGE ISLAND
Bainbridge Island, WA

Take a car-free adventure to Bainbridge Island by walking onto the ferry from downtown Seattle. The walk to the town is less than a quarter mile. Explore the Bainbridge Art Museum, enjoy great fish and chips at the Harbour Public House and pop into a wide array of art galleries and shops along Winslow Way E.

### 462 VASHON ISLAND
Vashon Island, WA

Vashon is a great day trip by ferry out of the Fauntleroy Dock in West Seattle. Don't miss hiking at Dockton Forest, eating at May Kitchen & Bar, or sightseeing at Point Robinson lighthouse.

### 463 BELLINGHAM
Bellingham, WA

There's an energy to college towns that's hard to describe, and Bellingham definitely has it. Spend your weekend in this small Northwest Washington city exploring breweries (Aslan and Kulshan are great), walking the South Bay Trail (an incredible boardwalk over the water), or checking out quirky museums like SPARK, the Museum of Electrical Invention.

## 464 MOUNT RAINIER NATIONAL PARK

Mount Rainier
National Park
*nps.gov/mora/
index.htm*

It would take a lifetime to explore all that Mount Rainier National Park has to offer, but if you only have one day, make it a weekday and drive up to either Sunrise or Paradise to explore the nearby trails, viewpoints and visitors centers. The Skyline Loop Trail (out of Paradise) is beyond spectacular. Wildflower season can last until August depending on when the snow melts, so pack your layers.

## 465 TACOMA

Tacoma, WA

Tacoma has a ton to offer as a destination in its own right, so feel free to tack on a few days to your trip to have enough time to explore the great parks, museums and restaurants. Point Defiance Park (and the aquarium within) has a great beach, killer views and ample hiking trails to wander.

464 MOUNT RAINIER NATIONAL PARK

# 5 worth-renting-a-car
# MULTI-DAY HIKES

### 466 MOOSE LAKE

47.9183, -123.3822
Olympic Peninsula
wta.org/go-hiking/
hikes/moose-lake

This pristine lake in the heart of Olympic National Park will have you driving to one of the most scenic trailheads in Washington state at Obstruction Point. You'll then descend into the lake basin, passing by a few other campsites along your way. Plan ahead to get permits through the National Park system, and then spend your days exploring nearby peaks and enjoy watching the light fade over the lake in the evenings.

### 467 SPRAY PARK LOOP

46.9330, -121.8643
Mount Rainier
National Park
wta.org/go-hiking/
hikes/spray-park-ipsut-
pass-loop

One of the most photographed viewpoints of Mount Rainier comes from Spray Park, but it takes some work to get there and to get permits to camp, so plan ahead. The Eagle's Roost campsite offers a great jumping-off point for a weekend of exploring. Bring your fully charged camera to capture *the* mountain in all her glory and keep your eyes open for brown bears feasting on ripening berries.

## 468 GREENWATER AND ECHO LAKES

47.1057, -121.4752
Enumclaw
wta.org/go-hiking/
hikes/greenwater-lakes

Is there anything more soothing than the sound of rushing water on a hike or while you're sleeping in a tent? This 14-mile trail (out-and-back) has several locations to pop your tent and enjoy one or a few evenings sleeping outside. Those who stay more than one night can use the same trail system to head to Coral Pass or Noble Knob for big views.

## 469 NAVAHO PEAK & PASS

47.3665, -120.8021
Teanaway
wta.org/go-hiking/
hikes/navaho-pass

This is a great earlier-season backpacking trip that doesn't require permits (but is a popular destination on weekends so come prepared). You'll traverse through what feels like six different types of subclimates on your way to the camping area five miles in. Drop your tent and heavier gear and head for the pass and Navaho Peak to enjoy spectacular views of the surrounding mountains.

## 470 CATHEDRAL PASS LOOP

48.8220, -120.0198
Pasayten Wilderness
wta.org/go-hiking/
hikes/cathedral-
pass-loop

This 44-mile trail through the heart of the Pasayten Wilderness traverses a particularly scenic section of the Boundary Trail, which in itself is a section of the Pacific Northwest Trail. While Cathedral Pass might be the highlight view of this long hike, there's plenty to look at and enjoy the whole time. Fire has ravaged this landscape over the last two decades; be sure to take note of nature's recovery efforts.

# 5 DAY HIKES

## *worth driving for*

### 471 CUTTHROAT PASS

48.5181, -120.7331
North Cascades
*wta.org/go-hiking/
hikes/cutthroat-pass-
via-pacific-crest-trail*

This stunning ten-mile hike is best accessed via the Pacific Crest Trail off of Highway 20. Keep your eyes open for PCT thru-hikers (this is the last leg for northbound hikers!) while you enjoy the variety of views from this trail. It's particularly worth traveling to in the fall, when western and subalpine larches turn the valley into a sea of golden pine needles.

### 472 EBEY'S LANDING

48.2049, -122.7060
Whidbey Island
*wta.org/go-hiking/
hikes/ebeys-landing*

This is an excellent spring or fall hike, when perhaps snow hasn't yet melted (or has already started falling) in the mountains. Enjoy incredible views of the Pacific Ocean, Olympic Mountains and San Juan Islands as you climb along a beach cliff and then hike down to return along the beach itself. There are excellent sea bird viewing opportunities along the way, but almost no shade so bring your sunscreen!

## 473 IRON BEAR — TEANAWAY RIDGE

47.3557, -120.7176
Central Cascades
*wta.org/go-hiking/
hikes/iron-bear*

This author makes an annual pilgrimage to Iron Bear & Teanaway ridge every year between Memorial Day and mid-June. The sunshine of the east side of the cascades is the perfect tonic for a cloudy Seattle spring weekend. Wildflowers to look out for include several varieties of paintbrush, balsamroot and red columbine. The views from the summit include the Stuart Ranger and Mount Rainier on a clear day.

## 474 MOUNT DICKERMAN

48.0538, -121.4900
Mountain Loop
Highway
*wta.org/go-hiking/
hikes/mount-dickerman*

This is a challenging day-hike but well worth the effort for the wide variety of views you'll encounter along the way. There are plenty of lower mileage and elevation hikes along the mountain loop highway, so you won't encounter large crowds on your journey. Along the way, keep your eye out for blueberries in summer, which aren't often found in the Cascades. Enjoy 360-degree views from the summit!

## 475 ANCIENT LAKES

47.1519, -119.9223
Quincy
*wta.org/go-hiking/
hikes/ancient-lakes*

Ancient Lakes is a great place to travel to if you want to appreciate just how varied Washington state's natural landscapes are. You'll feel as if you've been transported somewhere in the desert southwest, or on the set of the show *Westworld*. This arid landscape is a great place to dry out during Seattle's damp spring, but pack lots of water as there is none available on site.

473  IRON BEAR – TEANAWAY RIDGE

## 5 places to
# TRY A NEW HOBBY

**476 VERTICAL WORLD**

2330 W Commodore
Way
Magnolia ④
+1 206 283 4497
*verticalworld.com*

Vertical World is 'America's first climbing gym', with three locations to choose from in the Seattle area. They offer a wide variety of programs for adults and children, including weekly introductory classes for those just getting started. Gear can be rented on site and their online calendar makes it easy to see what events are happening on a daily basis.

**477 MOX BOARDING HOUSE**

5105 Leary
Avenue NW
Ballard ⑤
+1 206 523 9605
*moxboardinghouse.com*

Come to Mox Boarding House in Ballard the next time you want to try out a new board game before you buy it. Not only are their game store staff incredibly helpful at helping you select your next favorite game, you can hop next door to the bar and restaurant to try it out with friends or family while enjoying their pub fare and beverages.

### 478 FORT EBEY STATE PARK

400 Hill Valley Drive
Whidbey Island
+1 360 678 4636
parks.state.wa.us/507/
fort-ebey

This park has over 25 miles of multi-use trails that you can turn into a variety of loops by foot or bike. If you stayed the whole weekend (unless you're a marathon runner) it's unlikely that you'd have to walk the same trail twice (except to the bathroom of course). Come for the day or book a campsite to really get the most out of your explorations. Keep your eyes open on the bluff trails for whales feeding offshore.

### 479 GEARHOUSE

800 E Thomas St
Capitol Hill ③
+1 206 395 8790
joingearhouse.com

'Seattle's outdoor social club' just opened their second location on Capitol Hill, offering classes, social events and organized outdoor activities on a weekly basis. Whatever new outdoor hobby you're looking to try (kayaking, hiking, mountaineering, paddleboarding, cross-country skiing, the list goes on), they'll help you learn how and meet other people who are starting out.

### 480 POTTERY NORTHWEST

220 3rd Avenue S,
Lower Level
Pioneer Square ②
+1 206 209 1094
potterynorthwest.org

Pottery Northwest just opened a new space in the Pioneer Square neighborhood making it even easier to get the hang of throwing your own pottery. They offer a wide array of quarterly classes, workshops and memberships for those who would like regular studio access. They have plans to host their first gallery event in 2023. Tuition assistance is available.

## 5 of the best
# WINTER WEEKENDS

### 481 MOUNT BAKER
Glacier, WA

The small town of Glacier is a great place to use as a home base for winter adventures at the Mount Baker Ski area and beyond. Those who don't ski or snowboard can still enjoy incredible winter views with a four-mile snowshoe up to Artist Point, which offers incredible views of Mount Baker and surrounding mountains on a clear day. Chair 9 Pizza & Bar is the perfect *après*-stop on your way back to your rental cabin.

481 ARTIST POINT

## 482 LEAVENWORTH

Leavenworth, WA

This quirky Bavarian-themed town is worth a visit any time of year, but offers a particularly great jumping-off point for winter recreation at Stevens Pass Ski Area and the surrounding areas. The many German-inspired restaurants will satisfy your hearty winter appetites.

## 483 METHOW VALLEY

Mazama, WA

The small towns of Mazama, Winthrop and Twisp are a cross-country skiers' paradise. The Methow Trails System maintains 130 miles of groomed winter trails. The family-fun Mazama General Store is a must-visit.

## 484 WESTPORT

Westport, WA

Not many people think "let's go to the beach!" in the winter, but Westport is an idyllic fishing town to visit in the winter and you'll pay far less for oceanfront rental houses in the off-season. Bring your walking shoes to explore the beaches and Westport Light State Park at all hours of the day.

## 485 SEQUIM

Sequim, WA

The Olympic Peninsula has a very rainy reputation, but Sequim actually boasts more days of sunshine than the rest of Western Washington, thanks to its location right on the other side of the mountains and their rain shadow. Don't miss a visit to The Oak Table Cafe for breakfast and take a half day to explore Dungeness Spit Recreation Area & National Wildlife Refuge just north of town.

SEATTLE MONORAIL

# 15 RANDOM FACTS

5 great RESOURCES *(websites & other books)* — 262

5 *things to* KEEP IN MIND ———————— 264

5 BOOKS *and* MEDIA *starring Seattle* ———— 266

# 5 great **RESOURCES**
## *(websites & other books)*

---

### 486 **WASHINGTON TRAILS ASSOCIATION**
+1 206 625 1367
*wta.org*

If hiking is something you're thinking about doing while you're in Washington, definitely check out the Washington Trails Association (WTA) website and app, Trailblazer. They're the largest state-based hiking and trails focused organization in the country, with thousands of hikes to browse in their hiking guide and tons of tips on getting outside safely and responsibly.

### 487 **SEATTLE WALKS**
*uwapress.uw.edu/book/9780295741284/seattle-walks*

*Seattle Walks: Discovering History and Nature in the City* is a book absolutely worth buying for those interested in seeing the sights of Seattle on foot. Author David Williams offers a wide array of walks around the city that include both environmental, historical and architectural points of interest. It's refreshing to let yourself be guided by a book rather than a webpage for once.

## 488 VISIT SEATTLE
*visitseattle.org*

Visit Seattle is the city's nonprofit destination marketing organization, and a great place to start your planning process. They make it easy to find out about big events in the area and a visually inspiring social media presence to get you excited for your trip. They have a vast resource hub of things to do (in case the 500 tips in this book aren't quite enough!).

## 489 THE STRANGER
*thestranger.com*

*The Stranger* is a bi-weekly newspaper for the city of Seattle, founded in 1991 by the same person who founded the satirical newspaper, *The Onion*. While *The Stranger* isn't a satire newspaper, it is an offbeat news source and a great way to get a pulse on a part of the city's most progressive residents. They publish guides to local events and festivals as well as restaurant and cultural news in addition to current events.

## 490 *RECREATION.GOV*
*recreation.gov*

If you're looking to book a campsite or acquire a permit for a hike on federal land in Washington State, you'll have to use *recreation.gov* to do so. The website can be occasionally frustrating to use, but it's easier if you've already decided on a particular campsite (or general area) that you're interested in visiting. Get your inspiration on *wta.org* and then head to *recreation.gov* to make your reservations.

# 5 things to
# KEEP IN MIND

---

### 491 SEATTLE IS ON NATIVE LAND

*visitseattle.org/things-to-do/arts-culture/cultural-heritage/native-american*

Seattle, in addition to the entirety of the Pacific Northwest, sits on land forcibly stolen from Native Americans. Coast Salish tribes have stewarded this land since time immemorial, and local tribes continue to do so. We strongly recommend you spend some time learning about the city's original inhabitants either before or during your visit (or both!).

### 492 LET'S TALK ABOUT THE WEATHER

Seattle's weather has a rainy reputation that ultimately exceeds reality. Seattle doesn't rank in the top ten U.S. cities for total annual precipitation or number of rainy days. That being said, it is a pretty damp and gray place to visit from November-April when you definitely won't want to travel without a rain jacket. The lack of snow makes it an easy place to get around in the winter months, though, and Seattle Summer weather speaks for itself.

## 493 TRANSPORTATION TIPS

*tripplanner.kingcounty.gov/#/app/tripplanning*

Seattle's public transportation network isn't the worst you'll find, but it's not the most intuitive or streamlined either. The light rail from the airport will give you easy access to Columbia City, downtown, Capitol Hill and the University District, but bus transfers will be required to get you to neighborhoods west. Don't forget to check out the monorail that goes from downtown to Seattle Center or catch a ferry to a nearby destination!

## 494 RESTAURANT SERVICE IS... OKAY HERE

Seattle's restaurant scene has a glorious array of dining options, of which 85 are listed in this book. Unfortunately there can be a lack of friendly restaurant service at some mid-to-high-end restaurants. It won't ruin an otherwise good dining experience but it does make a friendly server stand out in the crowd.

## 495 SEATTLE'S HOMELESSNESS CRISIS

Seattle, like many American cities, has been faced with a growing population of people living on the streets over the last decade in addition to a growing crisis around mental health, which means some folks you come across on the streets of downtown Seattle might be visibly unwell. Purchasing a locally produced *Real Change* paper from a street vendor supports individuals and the organization working to empower folks into better economic conditions.

# 5 BOOKS *and* MEDIA
## *starring Seattle*

---

**496** *10 THINGS I HATE ABOUT YOU*
Gil Junger
1999

While the stunning high school filmed in this movie is actually in Tacoma, many of the other establishing shots for the movie were done on sight in Seattle. Familiar sites include the Fremont Troll, Kerry Park, Gas Works Park, Lake Union and even the Paramount Theatre. Definitely pop this movie on before your visit to Seattle to get excited about the many scenic spots you'll have to visit.

**497** *WHERE'D YOU GO BERNADETTE*
Maria Semple
2012

If you're trying to talk someone into visiting Seattle, don't necessarily let this book be the first thing you hand them for encouragement. A lasting memory from this author's reading of the novel was the detailed issue with blackberry bushes (an invasive plant wreaking havoc on our ecosystem here). But if you already love the city, read on, as the book fills in what it can feel like in the dark, gray winters here.

## 498 THE BOYS IN THE BOAT

Daniel James Brown
2013

This nonfiction book from Daniel James Brown is a great read for all, even those who might usually shy away from nonfiction. It follows the story of the nine Americans and University of Washington students who competed in the eight-oar crew team at the 1936 Berlin Olympics. It also paints a beautiful picture of the boys' upbringings across Washington and what it was like in Seattle during the Great Depression.

## 499 NATIVE SEATTLE

Coll Thrush
2017
uwapress.uw.edu/
book/9780295741345/
native-seattle

For those interested in learning more about Seattle's original inhabitants prior to your visit, pick up a copy of *Native Seattle* by Coll Thrush. The author explores how Native people have played an integral role in the development of the city of Seattle, and continue to do so to the present day. Be sure to pick up the most recent edition, updated in 2017.

## 500 SLEEPLESS IN SEATTLE

Nora Ephron
1993

This classic Nora Ephron film enchanted countless people into dreaming of living on a houseboat in Lake Union. You can still float by the original filming location in a kayak or paddleboard on the west side of Lake Union, though houseboats on both sides of the lake are beautiful to look at. When you visit the Athenian in Pike Place, keep your eyes open for a 'Tom Hanks Sat Here' plaque, too!

# INDEX

A1 Hop Shop   122
Ada's Technical Books
and Café   106
Add-a-Ball   94
Admiral Pub   96
Admiral Theater   196
Agua Verde Paddle Club   207
Aide-mémoire   139
Alibi Room   83
Alki Beach   158
Alki Kayak Tours   206
Ampersand Cafe on Alki   91
Ananya Spa Seattle   140
Ancient Lakes   254
Annapurna Cafe   42
AQUA by El Gaucho   37
Archie McPhee   119
Arctic Club Seattle   237
Ark Lodge Cinemas   196
Arthur's   56
Ascent Outdoors   108
Ba Bar Green   47
Bainbridge Island   248
Baker's   84
Bakery Nouveau   39
Bale Breaker & Yonder
Cider Taproom   90
Baleen   139
Ballard (Hiram M.
Chittenden) Locks   146
Ballard Carnegie
Library   145
Ballard Consignment
Store   130
Ballard Farmers Market   112
Ballard Locks
(fish ladder)   209
Ballard SeafoodFest   184
Baraka Gems   139
Bathtub Gin & Co   67

Bellingham   248
Benaroya Hall   178
Beveridge Place Pub   86
Bike rides   216, 217
Bill Speidels
Underground Tour   170
Billy Frank Jr. Nisqually
National Wildlife
Refuge   209
Biscuit Bitch   49
Black Bottle   28
*Black Sun*
by Isamu Noguchi   188
Blue Highway Games   225
Blue Poppy Floral   129
Boeing Factory:
Future of flight   126
Bon Voyage Vintage   135
Boombox Bar   97
booSH   127
Bottlehouse   68
Brouwer's Cafe   31
Browne Family Vineyards
Tasting Room   76
Bryant Corner Cafe   57
Buckley's   199
Bullitt Center   153
Bumbershoot   189
Burleskaraoke   99
Cafe Flora   47
Cafe Munir   46
Cafe Turko   40
Canon   67
Capitol Hill
Block Party   191
Capitol Hill
Farmers Market   112
Carkeek Park   203
Cathedral Pass Loop   252
Cedarbrook Lodge   243

Center for
Wooden Boats   149
Central Cinema   197
Chambers Bay   215
Changes Bar & Grill   101
Chihuly Garden
and Glass   177
Chinatown
Discovery Tours   170
Chuck's Hop Shop   75
ChuMinh Tofu   48
citizenM Seattle
South Lake Union   242
Ciudad   26
Clover Toys   225
Coffeeholic House   71
Colman Pool   210
Columbia City
Farmers Market   112
Communion   26
Corvus and Company   69
Couch   131
Creamy Cone Cafe   54
Crescent Lounge   101
Cutthroat Pass   253
Damn the Weather   85
Dark Horse Tattoo   136
Dash Point State Park   238
Daybreak Records   114
Daybreak Star
Cultural Center   194
DeLille Cellars   77
Denny Hall   144
Dick's Drive-In   50
Digs   130
Dimitriou's Jazz Alley   178
Dirty Harry's Balcony   204
Discovery Park
Loop Trail   202
Dockside Cannibas   117

Dockton Forest 205
Dough Joy 52
Driving Range at Jefferson
    Park Golf Course 214
Drumheller Fountain 161
Dumplings of Fury 44
Duwamish Longhouse
    and Cultural Center 194
Easy Street Records 113
Ebey's Landing 253
ECHO by Jaume Plensa 186
Eden Hill 44
Elliott Bay Book
    Company 106
Elliott Bay Brewpub 31
Elsom Cellars 77
Evergreen Point
    Floating Bridge 148
Ezell's Famous Chicken 60
Fairmont Olympic
    Hotel 243
FareStart Guest Chef
    Nights & Cafe 60
Fast Penny Spirits 126
Fat Cat Records 114
Fat's Chicken and Waffles 57
Fay Bainbridge Park 239
Feathered Friends 109
Filson 124
Fire Station No. 6 145
Fishing spots 212, 213
Flatstick Pub 95
Food Trucks 58, 59
Fort Ebey State Park 257
Four Seasons
    Hotel Seattle 211, 234
Freeman 133
Freeway Park 146
Fremont Brewery 90
Fremont Oktoberfest 169
Fremont Solstice
    Parade 185
Fremont Sunday
    Street Market 110
Fremont Vintage Mall 135
Frye Art Museum 193
Frélard Pizza Company 29

Full Throttle Bottles 123
Funko Pops 124
Gas Works Park 160
Gearhouse 257
Geocaching HQ 153
Georgetown Morgue 168
Georgetown Playfield
    Spray Park 210
Glasswing Shop 133
Gold Creek Trail
    at Green Mountain 205
Golden Gardens 159
Good Day Donuts 52
Graduate Seattle 235
Grand Illusion Cinema 197
Green Lake Boathouse
    & Coffee Shop 207
Green Lake
    Jewelry Works 138
Green Lake Loop 163
Green Lake Pitch
    & Putt 227
Greenwater and
    Echo Lakes 252
Growlerz Taproom 93
Habitude 141
Hammering man by
    Jonathan Borofsky 188
Harbor City 57
Hat n' Boots 155
Hattie's Hat 72
Hello Robin 54
Henry Art Gallery 192
Hibulb Cultural
    Center & Natural
    History Preserve 194
Holy Mountain
    Brewing Company 80
Homer 43
Hotel Ballard 236
Hotel Max 237
Hothouse Spa & Sauna 141
How to Cook a Wolf 35
Husky Deli & Ice Cream 53
Hyatt at Olive 8 243
Hyatt Regency Seattle 243
Ice Box Arcade 95

Indigenous People
    Festival 185
Iron Bear –
    Teanaway Ridge 254
Jackstraw Inc 133
Jefferson Park 228
Jerk Shack 46
Jetty Island Park 159
Joule 35
Julia's on Broadway 97
Jupiter Bar 95
Kasala Outlet 131
Kedai Makan 28
Kemp's Weed Shop 118
Kerry Park 160
KiDiMu 223
Kids Flight Zone @
    Museum of Flight 223
Kids Inflatable Fun Zone 227
King Donuts 51
Klondike Gold
    Rush National
    Historical Park 151, 171
Kremwerk 96
Kubota Garden 165
KushKlub 118
Lake Sammamish
    State Park 211
Lake Serene & Bridal
    Veil Falls 205
Lake Union
    Hot Tub Boats 207
Lake Union Park Bridge 148
Lakeridge Park Loop 203
Larch-Marching 169
Lark 44
Laughing Buddha
    Seattle 137
Liberty 68
Lil Red Takeout
    and Catering 46
Lincoln Park 208, 220
Linda's Tavern 61
List Restaurant 28
Little Red Hen 98
Llandover Woods 203
London Bridge Studio 179

| | |
|---|---|
| Lottie's Lounge | 86 |
| Lowman Park Beach | 159 |
| Lucky Dog Clothing | 134 |
| Macrina Bakery & Cafe | 38 |
| Madison Park Beach | 159 |
| Mama Sambusa Kitchen | 42 |
| Mammoth | 49 |
| Marination Ma Kai | 88 |
| Mashiko | 36 |
| Matthews Beach Park | 210 |
| mbar | 88 |
| McMenamins Six Arms | 33 |
| Meeples Games | 121 |
| Meskel | 60 |
| Metier Brewing | |
| Company Taproom | 80 |
| Michael Birawer Gallery | 192 |
| Middle Fork | |
| Campground | 239 |
| Mighty-O donuts | 51 |
| Milstead & Co. | 70 |
| Mimosas Cabaret | 97 |
| Molly Moon's Homemade | |
| Ice Cream | 54 |
| Montlake Bridge | 148 |
| Moose Lake | 251 |
| MoPOP Museum | 155, 176, 178 |
| Mount Dickerman | 254 |
| Mount Rainier | |
| National Park | 249 |
| Mox Boarding House | 256 |
| My Three Little Birds | 224 |
| Mystery Made Co. | 132 |
| National Nordic | |
| Museum | 177 |
| Navaho Peak & Pass | 252 |
| New Luck Toy | 69 |
| New Year's Day Bonfire | 173 |
| Nielsen's Pastries | 39 |
| Nightfall Orphanage | 168 |
| Northwest Art & Frame | 115 |
| Northwest Folklife | |
| Festival | 191 |
| Northwest Native Art | 195 |
| Northwest Outdoor | |
| Center | 206 |
| Old Stove Brewing | 93 |

| | |
|---|---|
| Open Books A Poem | |
| Emporium | 107 |
| Orient Express | 99 |
| Ounces Taproom | |
| & Beer Garden | 74 |
| Outdoor Research | 109 |
| Outer Space Seattle | 227 |
| OZ. Cannabis | 118 |
| Pacific Inn Pub | 36 |
| Pacific Science Center | 226 |
| Paper Boat Booksellers | 107 |
| Paramount Theatre | 180 |
| Perihelion Brewery | 33 |
| Phnom Penh | |
| Noodle House | 40 |
| Photographic Center | |
| Northwest | 115 |
| Pike & Western | 123 |
| Pike Place Market | 182, 183 |
| Pike St. Press | 126 |
| Pioneer Square | |
| Totem Pole | 151 |
| Piroshky Piroshky | 183 |
| Plum Bistro | 48 |
| Polish Home Association | |
| Friday Night Dinners | 42 |
| Pony | 101 |
| Portage Bay | 30 |
| Portalis Wine Shop | 123 |
| Pottery Northwest | 257 |
| Pretty Parlor | 135 |
| Prism | 121 |
| Queen Mary Tea Room | 70 |
| Quinn's Pub | 85 |
| Radiator Whiskey | 45 |
| Ray's Boathouse | 87 |
| REI Flagship Store | 109 |
| Reuben's Brews | 79 |
| Ridgewood Bottle & Tap | 75 |
| Rock Box | 98 |
| RockCreek Seafood | |
| & Spirits | 37 |
| Rookies Sports Bar | |
| and Grill | 199 |
| Rough & Tumble Pub | 198 |
| Roxhill Park | 221 |
| Ruckus Recreational | 117 |

| | |
|---|---|
| Sacred Rain | |
| Healing Center | 140 |
| Salish Lodge & Spa | 240 |
| Salmon Bay Park | 221 |
| Saltwater State Park | 239 |
| Salty's on Alki | 61 |
| Schilling Cider House | 74 |
| Schmitz Preserve Park | 202 |
| Sea Monster Lounge | 181 |
| Seafair | 184 |
| Seahurst Park | 229 |
| Seattle Aquarium | 222 |
| Seattle Architecture | |
| Foundation | 152 |
| Seattle Art Museum | 177 |
| Seattle Bouldering | |
| Project | 227 |
| Seattle Center | 229 |
| Seattle Children's | |
| Museum | 222 |
| Seattle Children's | |
| PlayGarden | 221 |
| Seattle Christmas | |
| Boat Parade | 173 |
| Seattle International | |
| Film Festival | 189 |
| Seattle Japanese Garden | 165 |
| Seattle Marriott | |
| Waterfront | 234 |
| Seattle Plant Daddy | 129 |
| Seattle Public Library: | |
| Central Library | 154 |
| Seattle Queer | |
| Film Festival | 191 |
| Seattle Tavern | |
| & Pool Hall | 94 |
| Seattle's Best Karaoke | 99 |
| September Shop | 132 |
| Serendipity Cafe | 30 |
| Serious Pie | 34 |
| Seven Hills | |
| Running Shop | 116 |
| Seward Park Outer Loop | 228 |
| s'gwi gwi ? altxw: | |
| House of Welcome | 195 |
| Side Quest Tattoo | 137 |
| SIFF Cinema Egyptian | 197 |

Silver Platters SoDo 114
Skagit Valley
    Tulip Festival 166
Smith Tower 149
Smith Tower
    Observatory Bar 87
Snapdoodle
    Toys & Games 224
SODO Urbanworks 75
Some Random Bar 83
Sonic Boom Records 114
Space Needle 151
Spinasse 43
Spray Park Loop 251
Stampede Cocktail Club 67
Standard Goods 119
Starbucks Reserve
    Roastery 71
Steinbrueck
    Native Gallery 193
Stimson-Green Mansion 152
Stitches 116
Stonington Gallery 193
Storm Bloom Tattoo 137
Stoup 79
Stuhlbergs 121
Sugarlump 225
Sully's Snow
    Goose Saloon 73
Swansons Nursery 127
Syttende Mai 185
Taco Time NW 49
Tacoma 249
Taku 34
Targy's Tavern 73
Taylor Shellfish
    Oyster Bar 36
TeKu Tavern + Cafe 69
The 5 Point Cafe 72
The Alki Homestead 145
The Athenian Seafood
    Restaurant and Bar 84
The Barn Owl
    Vintage Goods 134
The Beer Junction 122
The Coupe & Flute 57
The Crocodile 181

The Cuff Complex 100
The Dock Sports
    Bar & Grill 199
The Edgewater Hotel 234
The Egg & Us 30
The Flour Box 39
The George & Dragon
    Pub 198
The Golf Club
    at Newcastle 214
The Good Society Brewery
    & Public House 80
The Heathman Hotel 237
The Inn at the Market 236
The Ladies Room 141
The Lodge at St. Edward 241
The Lookout 88
The Nook 66
The Pike Brewing
    Company 33
The Princess & Bear 77
The Rooftop Boardwalk
    at T-Mobile Park 160
The Royal Room 179
The Showbox 181
The Spheres 154
The Troll by Steve
    Badanes & Team 186
The Velvet Elk 86
The Walrus &
    the Carpenter 35
The Wayward Vegan 48
The Wingluke Museum 176
The Woodmark
    Hotel & Still 241
The Works 116
Theatre Tours 153
Theo Chocolate 53
Third Place Books 107
Thompson Seattle 235
Three Tree Point B&B 240
Tinte Cellars 76
Tirto Furniture 131
Tolt MacDonald Park
    & Campground 238
Top Pot Doughnuts 51
Tractor Tavern 181

Treehouse Point 240
True Love Tattoo
    & Art Gallery 136
True Northwest:
    The Seattle Journey 171
Umami Kushi 39
Un Bien 50
Underwater Dome 171
Unexpected Productions
    Improv 183
Union Bay Natural Area 209
Uptown Espresso 71
Valerie Madison 138
Vashon Island 248
Vertical World 256
Viengthong Lao
    Restaurant 46
Volunteer Park 229
Von's 1000 Spirits 84
Waiting for the Interurban
    by Richard Beyer 188
Wallace Falls State Park 205
Ward House 145
Washington National
    Golf Club 215
Washington Park
    Arboretum 166
Washington State Fair 169
Waterfall Garden Park 154
Wedgwood Ale House
    & Cafe 73
West Seattle
    Farmers Market 110
West Seattle Golf Course 215
West Seattle Nursery
    & Garden Center 129
West Seattle Water Taxi 161
Westcrest Park 220
Wetlands at
    Golden Gardens 208
WildRose 100
Wing Dome 30
Wonderland
    Gear Exchange 109
Woodland Park Zoo 223
Zig Zag Cafe 66
Zoo Lights 173

# COLOPHON

EDITING *and* COMPOSING — Allie Tripp — alliestripp.com

GRAPHIC DESIGN — Joke Gossé and doublebill.design

PHOTOGRAPHY — Allie Tripp

ADDITIONAL PHOTOGRAPHY — p. 27, 32, 38, 55, 62-63, 78, 167, 235, 241: Alena Sullivan — burnashburn.com

COVER IMAGE — Pike Place Market (secrets 321–325)
© artworks shown on image p. 174: Courtesy of Chihuly Garden and Glass

The addresses in this book have been selected after thorough independent research by the author, in collaboration with Luster Publishing. The selection is solely based on personal evaluation of the business by the author. Nothing in this book was published in exchange for payment or benefits of any kind.

The author and the publisher have made every effort to obtain permission for all illustrations and to list all copyright holders. Interested parties are requested to contact the publisher.

D/2023/12.005/21
ISBN 978 94 6058 3476
NUR 510, 513

© 2023 Luster Publishing, Antwerp
lusterpublishing.com — THE500HIDDENSECRETS.COM
info@lusterpublishing.com

Printed in Italy by Printer Trento.

MIX
Paper | Supporting responsible forestry
FSC® C015829
www.fsc.org